Buddhism in the Light of Christ

Buddhism in the Light of Christ

A Former Buddhist Nun's Reflections,
with Some Helpful Suggestions on How to Reach Out
to Your Buddhist Friend

ESTHER BAKER

RESOURCE *Publications* · Eugene, Oregon

Resource Publications
An Imprint of Wipf and Stock Publishers
199 W. 8th Ave., Suite 3
Eugene, OR 97401

www.wipfandstock.com

ISBN 13: 978-1-62564-466-4

Manufactured in the U.S.A.   04/15/2014

Unless otherwise identified, Scripture quotations are taken from New International
Version. Copyright © 1979, 1984, 2011 by Biblica, formerly International Bible
Society.

Scripture quotations marked nkjv are taken from the New King James Version.
Copyright © 1979, 1980, 1982 by Thomas Nelson, Inc.

Scripture quotations marked esv are taken from The Holy Bible, English Standard
Version® (ESV®), copyright © 2001 by Crossway, a publishing ministry of Good
News Publishers.

Scripture quotations marked nasb are taken from the NEW AMERICAN STAN-
DARD BIBLE®, Copyright © 1960,1962,1963,1968,1971,1972,1973,1975,1977,1995
by The Lockman Foundation. Used by permission.

"The Tree" Illustration copyright © Jenny Daymond 2014

"Return, . . .," says the Lord, "Return to Me"; . . . "Then you shall not be moved." (from Jer 4:1 nkjv)

Contents

Illustrations

Foreword

Buddhism in the Light of Christ tells an important adventure of seeking truth in the modern era. For many years Esther Baker was a dedicated Buddhist nun. Her deep involvement with Buddhism in both Thailand and the United Kingdom brings a veritable ring of reality to the pages of her new book. Esther shares honestly her experiences and insights of those years through the enlightening lens of someone who has genuinely come to know Christ. Her journey is an intriguing one, filled with revealing lessons regarding two of the world's great dominant religions, Buddhism and Christianity. Her testimony of personal struggles and her openly sharing about inner conceptual conflicts are commendable. Here is a practical tool to help educate Christians about Buddhism, as well as for Buddhists to learn about Christ. Esther's gifted attention to detail is mellowed by her simple style of writing. She tells her stories with beneficial explanation of key Buddhist terms and meanings. Her analyses of concepts are illustrated by real life examples and couched in cogent terms that are easily comprehensible.

To the classical minds of academic pundits her descriptions of Buddhism, as she has experienced it more recently as a Christian missionary in Asia, may seem to be simplistic or even questionable at times. However, the majority of more than one billion Buddhists in the twenty-first century follow variegated forms of folk Buddhism sometimes called peoples' Buddhism. It is this down-to-earth Buddhism that the local people believe and follow, which Esther explains here, more often than the pristine tenets expounded by the Buddha in the sixth century before Christ. While its followers have integrated other religious elements from their indigenous cultures, it is no less dedicated to Buddhism. Indeed, wherever Buddhism enters a new culture it espouses that spiritual environment, changing color like an adapting chameleon. The Tibetan forms incorporated ancient Bon spirits and Shamanism. The Japanese blended the Shinto nature spirits with

Buddhism. South East Asian Theravada Buddhists combined animism, shamanistic practices, ancestral cults, and Brahman ceremonies and spiritual entities into their various expressions of popular folk Buddhism.

This book contributes to educating the church on Buddhist beliefs. It helps to awaken the clear vision to understand the variety of many Asian Buddhists in our communities today; challenging Christians to reach out to them with the Gospel of Christ's compassion. Furthermore, Esther's scintillating reflection assists the church to be aware of the growing tendency for westerners to become involved with ancient Eastern religions like Buddhism or dabble in New Age practices. Pastors, elders, deacons, Sunday school teachers, missionaries—in fact most Christians—will profit from studying this tome.

Enjoy reading it thoughtfully.

Dr. Alex G. Smith
OMF International
Portland Oregon, USA
November 1, 2013

Acknowledgments

So many people have contributed to the birth of this book, both directly and indirectly. I am truly grateful to you all. So, we ask: please fulfill your holy purposes through it Lord, in Jesus' name. Amen.

Although these stories are true, many of the names of people and places have been changed.

My perspective on Buddhism comes from my experience of the Thai Theravāda tradition. Other forms of Buddhism may have different beliefs and practices from those described here.

Regarding the use of diacritical marks for the Pali language, I have followed the spelling as found in *What the Buddha Taught* by Walpola Sri Rahula.

Introduction

Truly thankful as I am to have told my story in *I Once Was a Buddhist Nun*, I felt clearly that there was more I wanted to share. So, I am very happy to introduce this book to you, its sequel and companion.

In *I Once . . .* , I tell my story of how I was brought up in England, where in my family the idea of going to church was little more than a joke. Then, at the age of twenty one, my spiritual side, which for the most part had been suppressed, suddenly erupted like a volcano, marking the beginning of my focused and lasting quest in search of truth.

Shortly after, I encountered Buddhism which quickly caught my interest and gained my increasing commitment. I was particularly drawn to the Theravāda tradition, the southern school of Buddhism found in countries such as Thailand, Sri Lanka, and Cambodia.

In all, I was a Buddhist for more than thirteen years. Seven-and-a-half of those I spent as a Buddhist nun, receiving two ordinations, first as a novice and then as a "ten precept" nun, going ever deeper into meditation and detachment from the world. Living like this—under the penetrating influence of Buddhism—profoundly changed my understanding of both the world and myself.

That was until God wondrously met with me inside the Buddhist temple and revealed to me that Jesus, his Son, *was* the truth I had been searching for. He drew me to himself and out of Buddhism completely, demolishing the power of my longstanding belief in it even while I was still in the Buddhist robe!

That was more than twenty two years ago. Since then, I have been a missionary in Hong Kong for three years in the 1990s, and from 2000 I have been based in the Buddhist nation of Thailand where I have been involved in helping to establish a Christian ministry that has discipleship as its core purpose. We aim to help all kinds of Thai Christians from church leaders to new believers to mature in their faith; usually working in teams.

Buddhism is well established in some parts of Asia, where it has a long history, and now it has quietly infiltrated the West, too. We are aware of its presence in various ways, from glossy travel magazines with romanticized photos of temples in Burma to statues of Buddha on sale in furniture and charity shops to (more seriously) a new wave of therapy involving "mindfulness"— taken directly from Buddhist insight meditation—that has impacted the counseling world and entered mainstream psychology.

But, whether in the East or the West, in its traditional or its folk expressions, what is Buddhism? What is at the heart of its teachings? How does it differ from Christianity, and is it compatible with it? Ever elusive and hard to grasp, like a slippery fish, I realize that Buddhism remains a mystery to many people, including Christians.

In this book, I take a brief look at the Buddha's teachings and then share a collection of short stories, testimonies, and reflections, both mine and other people's, covering a number of topics. My prayer is that they will help you to see how Buddhism reflects in the light of Christ, and that this will deepen your understanding of its true nature. And, in helping to demystify it, this will better equip you to address the influence of Buddhism in the world around you.

I am aware, too, that many Christians have a relative or friend who is involved in Buddhism to some degree. I am often asked how to help them, and so I offer some suggestions on how to share the gospel, the uniqueness of Jesus, with them. I also point out some important considerations regarding discipleship once a Buddhist has come to Christ.

Chapter 1

Basic Teachings of the Buddha

"I am the way." (Words of Jesus, John 14:6)

We will be visiting Asia later, but let's begin by considering the fascination Buddhism holds for some westerners, even though they were not born into it and it has never been part of their original culture.

David, an English friend of mine, shares his story:

"In my late twenties, I felt there must be more to life than the daily grind of 9 to 5 and the rampant materialism of those around me. The view most people seemed to have—you're born, you work to accumulate lots of things to make you happy, then you die—just wasn't satisfying, and I was looking for something more spiritual. I'd studied science at university and have always had an active, enquiring mind with lots of questions about life—some quite unsettling, like 'Where do we come from?' and 'What happens when we die?' I knew that things were not as they should be in my life.

"One day I spotted a notice about meditation and remembered going to a relaxing class years before; so I went along. It was run by a group of Buddhists belonging to [what was then called] the Friends of the Western Buddhist Order. They were friendly and welcoming; I liked that the teaching made me think, and I found that the meditation gave me a feeling of peace and was helpful for putting aside the unease I had with some of those big questions.

"As time went by, I found myself drawn more into meditation and started practicing at home, particularly meditation on the breath, working to clear my mind of everything.

"Over a couple of years, I was involved in ceremonies and a retreat, but I didn't feel comfortable with everything I was doing and didn't really feel like myself. Going further with Buddhist practices would mean giving up things I wasn't prepared to give up. Not just little things but even my own name—in a sense, my identity! I was taught that this world is not real, it's a delusion, and that this was why it didn't really make sense. Through meditation I was trying to escape from the world with all its problems, but when it came down to it I just couldn't let go.

"I had many questions to ask about the nature of reality, but as time went by I found that the more I learnt about Buddhism, the more questions I had. Just as I was beginning to grasp things, it seemed they were even harder to grasp and further away.

"Then, one time at the Buddhist center, something unusual happened during a meditation session. I could see in my mind a beautiful glow coming from a fire in a cave. Nothing odd about that—often in meditation I had various images and sensations. However, it was unusual to see people, and on this occasion I saw a man wearing a white robe on the other side of the fire, looking at me, smiling. I felt amazingly at peace. Suddenly the bell rang, calling us out of meditation. When I asked one of the Buddhist leaders what my experience could mean, he just said it was 'very auspicious.' *What was the real meaning of this*, I wondered?

"A couple of weeks later, walking around a country church and enjoying the feeling of peace, I sensed a voice calling me to 'come back.' I had a sudden memory of the man in the cave. I'd been to church as a child and had believed in God, but I'd lost that for various reasons. Now, standing in the church, I had the incredible realization that the man in the meditation had been Jesus—and *this* voice was his. I had no idea what to do and mulled it over for some days.

"At a party soon afterwards, I met Cathy, a lovely Christian lady, and some of her Christian friends. I mentioned the meditation experience and the voice and started asking them questions, which they were only too happy to answer. Each question was met with a clear, honest, and, above all, compelling response. I was convinced I had to take another look at Christianity.

"Over time, I became increasingly sure that Buddhism was not the way for me. As I got to know Cathy better, I learned more about her faith. One day, she invited me to her church. During the sermon I suddenly realized that it was true: Jesus is *the* way. I'd been trying to escape from the world, but God wanted me to stop doing that and to engage with the world and embrace all that he had for me. I gave my life to Christ that day and haven't looked back. I've never done any more Buddhist meditation and don't miss it.

"About a year later Cathy became my wife, and, ever since, God has taken us on an amazing journey together. He's always with us. I know that life isn't just 9 to 5, and I now embrace the real meaning God gives to it. I'm involved in workplace outreach, have been on mission, and have had opportunities to preach. And those questions? I know that God has all the answers. Whether he answers them all or not now, I know I can trust him."

I find David's story a beautiful one—quite a turnaround and with a happy ending, too!

Westerners are drawn to Buddhism in different ways. For many like David, beginning to meditate can be a significant first step toward a personal identification with it and deeper commitment to it. Others find its subtle and refined philosophy appealing. Some are intrigued by distant countries and cultures, such as Tibet, and want to experience for themselves something of what the people there believe.

Once we have opened the door to Buddhism though—whichever door it may be—it's easy to be gently persuaded by it and drawn in, whereby our outlook and worldview can be transformed, incredibly almost unnoticed at times. That was certainly my experience—until finally wanting to give it my all.

Traditionally, becoming a Buddhist involves taking refuge in the Buddha, Dhamma (Buddha's teaching), and Sangha (the Buddhist community—the order of monks and nuns).

In what David shares, I can see some common factors that often seem to have applied to many westerners I've known who have been attracted to Buddhism, including me.

Here is a list of some of them. It's quite general, and we do not find all of these in David's story.

Buddhism may appeal to westerners who are spiritually:

- disillusioned or disappointed with the church, many having had some degree of contact with it in the past

- skeptical about Christianity, seeing it as hypocritical, pharisaical, and irrelevant

- reacting at some level against and/or are in rebellion to God, and so are not interested in a faith that requires belief in him

- open to and interested in spiritual alternatives such as Eastern religions and New Age (many New Age practices have their roots in Eastern philosophy) which many expressions of Buddhism can easily accommodate
- attracted to meditation that offers "inner peace, escape, and healing"
- drawn to the idea of stilling and/or emptying their overstimulated and overactive minds
- wanting to quiet and simplify often complex, busy lives

looking for a way out or help to cope with personal difficulties and/or the problems of the world

Personality traits of westerners attracted to Buddhism may include:
- being independent and self-sufficient
- having a searching, enquiring mind, and often a bright intellect—Buddhism appeals to the mind, it is intellectually engaging
- being kind, compassionate, and attracted to peace and gentleness
- having an existing (sometimes deep) familiarity with feeling empty and detached and being unsure of who they are
- feeling that withdrawing is a place of safety (perhaps from childhood)
- at some level feeling disconnected from people; i.e., from key figures in life
- feeling tired of the materialistic, consumerist, "rat-race" society
- at some level feeling unfulfilled by or dissatisfied with worldly things
- wanting association with like-minded people

You may wonder, then, how many practicing Buddhists there are in the West. Contrary to what many people imagine, the actual number remains small, though interest seems to be growing. Statistics can vary—it is notoriously difficult to get accurate figures—but it is estimated that only 0.4 percent of the British population is Buddhist[1] and 0.7 percent of the population of the United States.[2]

These figures include Buddhists who have emigrated from Buddhist countries. But regarding non-Christian westerners, I think the spiritual

---

1. www.secularbuddhism.co.uk/2012/12/2011-census-statistics; Wikipedia, "Religion in the United Kingdom," February 2014.

2. Wikipedia, "Buddhism in the United States," February 2014.

hunger some have can provoke them to enjoy flirting with Buddhist thinking and terminology, but on closer inspection they find that it's simply far too different to their way of thinking and cannot take it that seriously—hence the low numbers.

Out of the global population of about seven billion, more than one billion are estimated to be Buddhists (this number is made up mainly of folk Buddhists which we will read more of later), making (folk) Buddhism the world's third-largest religion.[3]

The number of Christians—including all denominations: Roman Catholic, Protestant, Eastern Orthodox, etc.—is estimated to make up approximately one third of the world's population, making it the largest world religion.[4] Interestingly, over the last few decades there has been incredible growth in Christian populations in places like China, Africa, and South America, to the point that there are now many more Christians living outside the West than in it.

So, who was the Buddha? He was a man, not a figure of myth or legend, born in the sixth century bc; a prince from a Hindu ruling family which lived in the Himalayan foothills, then part of northern India but now in Nepal. His personal name was Siddhattha (Pali; Siddhārtha in Sanskrit), and his family name was Gotama (Skt. Gautama). He enjoyed a life of luxury and, according to the custom of the time, married a beautiful princess at the young age of sixteen. He had an unusual, very sheltered life—his father wanted to protect him from the harsher realities of life.

However, he was curious to know what lay beyond the protective walls of the palace, and so he escaped outside with his charioteer. On his travels, he saw for the first time an old person, a sick person, a dead body, and a monk. Having never seen these "signs" before, he was deeply impacted when faced with the reality of human suffering, sickness, and death. *As a result, a profound desire arose in him to find the way out of suffering, which became the principal motivation in his spiritual search.*

Soon afterwards, at the age of twenty nine and not long after the birth of his son—whom he named Rāhula (meaning "chain" or "fetter")—Gotama escaped the palace again, leaving his family to become an ascetic, living a simple, strict way of life in search of answers.

---

3. Smith, *A Christian's Pocket Guide to Buddhism*, 7.

4. Wikipedia, "List of Religious Populations," February 2014.

For six years he wandered about the Ganges valley, following local religious teachers and going through various rigorous ascetic practices such as self denial and self mortification, sometimes fasting to an extreme. This didn't give him the understanding he was searching for, so he abandoned such known methods to find his own way.

One evening, at the age of thirty five, with his focus on finding an end to suffering, he sat down under a fig tree near a river in northern India and meditated. There, he had an extreme and unusual experience which became known as "enlightenment" or nirvāṇa. It remains the goal of Buddhism to this day. After this, he became known as Buddha.

Soon afterwards, he began to teach his philosophical insights he had under the tree. Before long, some men and women wanted to follow him, and so the order of Buddhist monks and nuns came into being. He spent much time in meditation, incorporating various ascetic practices into his daily life and travelled far and wide across India, teaching all kinds of people for forty-five years. He died at the age of eighty and was cremated.

The Buddha's teachings were first written down in Pali, the ancient Indian language that he used, in Ceylon (present-day Sri Lanka) in the first century ad. They make up the *Tipiṭaka* (in Pali; *Tripiṭaka* in Sanskrit) or "three baskets" of Theravāda Buddhism: *Sutta*, the discourses of the Buddha; *Abhidharma*, the philosophical and psychological aspect of Buddhist doctrine; and *Vinaya*, the rules of monastic life.

In Buddha's teachings, we can see an influence of Hinduism. Having been born a Hindu, he absorbed some of its beliefs such as karma and rebirth, but rejected others.

Buddha never claimed to be God, or a little "god" even; simply a human being. He did not recognize creator God or any higher being or power to answer to. Rather, he considered the position of human beings to be "supreme," where each is their own "master." He sought knowledge and understanding through mere human effort; his insights were based on his intelligence, rational mind, and personal endeavor.

Buddha admitted that he could not help anyone; only point the way. As we read in Walpola Sri Rahula's well known and respected book on Theravāda Buddhism, *What the Buddha Taught* (to which I shall often refer), Buddha taught that every person should "be a refuge to themselves";[5] not to seek help or refuge from others but through their own efforts work

5. Rahula, *What the Buddha Taught*, 1.

out their emancipation. To me, this helps explain the appeal of Buddhism to those more independent minded people who have no place for God.

It is fitting that Buddha is referred to as a "scientific doctor,"[6] as his teachings and meditation practices tended to come more from his mind and intellect, rather than from his heart—an approach that was often clinical and analytical. For example, a common theme in his style of teaching was to analyze and break down mental and physical phenomena—such as feelings, a human being, a chariot—into their component parts and list them. By breaking them down in this way, Buddha assumed that he had proven their inherent emptiness and insubstantiality by claiming that they were no more than the listed parts.

Buddhism is vast and complex, but here is a brief, and by no means complete, summary of the basic teachings often to be found at the heart of various forms of Buddhism:

- the four noble truths
- the five aggregates
- karma and rebirth
- the three characteristics of existence
- meditation

The four noble truths that Buddha taught in his first sermon, explaining the insights he had had under the fig tree, are:

1. suffering (*dukkha*)
2. the origin of suffering (*samudaya*)
3. the cessation of suffering (*nirodha*)
4. the way leading to the cessation of suffering (*magga*)

To expand on these briefly:

1. Buddha's view of life and the world was that everything is imperfect and insubstantial. Quoting E. Stanley Jones (1884–1973), an American Methodist missionary and theologian who served in India: "He went further than saying that there is suffering in existence. The Buddha said that suffering and existence are fundamentally and inextricably one."[7]

6. Ibid., 17.

7. 4. Smith, referring to E. Stanley Jones, *Christ and Human Suffering*, New York: Abingdon-Cokebury 1933, 47, quoted in De Neui, *Suffering*, 62.

2. Buddha concluded that the cause of suffering is desire, craving, and attachment, which he claimed led to future births. He taught of karma which he said perpetuates an endless cycle of being reborn into various "realms": human, animal, ghost, heavens (plural) and hells (plural).

3. The cessation of suffering he saw as the elimination of desire, craving, and attachment.

4. He claimed that this would come about through following his "middle path" which, he said, "avoids two extremes: the search for happiness through the pleasures of the senses [and] the search for happiness through self- mortification in different forms of asceticism."[8] This "middle path" is generally referred to as "the noble eightfold path," being composed of eight categories.

This, Buddha said, would lead to nirvāṇa or "Extinction,"[9] the final release from being born. Much of Buddha's teaching deals in one way or another with this path.

Buddha divided a human being into five aggregates (*pañcakkhandha*):

1. matter (*rūpakkhandha*)

2. sensations (*vedanākkhandha*)

3. perceptions (*saññākkhandha*)

4. mental formations (*saṃkhārakkhandha*)

5. consciousness (*viññāṇakkhandha*)

For karma and rebirth, please see chapter 4, "Karma and Grace."

Buddha taught that all phenomena whether physical or mental have three characteristics, they are: impermanent (*anicca*), unsatisfactory or prone to suffering (*dukkha*), and not belonging to a self or soul (*anatta*). Please see chapter 5, "Impermanence, Suffering, No Self, or True Self," for more on these.

He also taught various meditation practices—ways of focusing the mind—such as "loving kindness" and the contemplation of death. Two significant ones are "concentration" (*samādhi*) and "insight" meditation (*vipassanā*)—an analytical method based on mindfulness and awareness. Chapter 3, "Meditation and Prayer," will look into this further.

Buddhist meditation practice forms a significant part of the path aiming for nirvāṇa.

8. Rahula, op. cit., 45.

9. Ibid., 36.

From its beginnings in ancient India, Buddhism later spread south to countries such as Sri Lanka, Thailand, Laos, Cambodia, and Burma, forming what is known as the Southern or Theravāda school of Buddhism, and north to China, Mongolia, Korea, and Japan, forming the Northern or Mahāyāna school of Buddhism.

It is in this part of the world that Buddhism has really put down its roots, being the predominant religion of countries such as Sri Lanka, Thailand, and (formerly) Tibet for centuries now. Its impact has permeated deeply into language, thinking, lifestyle, culture, and even national identity. For instance, for most of the people of Thailand, Laos, and Burma, to be Thai, Laos, or Burmese is to be Buddhist.

The development of Buddhism in the course of its wide travels and over time reveals its somewhat mercurial nature. By this I mean that Buddhism possesses a great ability to adapt to different cultures and integrate into them. A big part of that is in its absorption and assimilation of certain local beliefs and indigenous religions along its way, while often maintaining its dominance over them (one clear exception to this being genuine Christianity). These may include the worship of spirits, idols, and ancestors, and the practice of the occult, all of which contain a "family resemblance" to Buddhism and often sit comfortably alongside one other, as we shall explore later.

Such assimilation significantly aided the spread of Buddhism by making it far more readily acceptable, and in doing so has led to an unbelievable number and variety of Buddhist groups, practices, and cults.

This eclectic spiritual mix is often known as folk Buddhism or the peoples' Buddhism and makes up *by far* the majority of Buddhists in the world. While those who adhere strictly to the traditional form of Buddhism (referring to the official teachings, beliefs, and practices of Buddhism) make up a small minority.

Dr. Alex Smith, a former long-term missionary to Thailand, has observed: "Buddhist thinking, mixed with animistic beliefs, still pervades much of the Asian worldview today."[10] Interestingly however, such assimilated spiritual practices as are found in folk Buddhism are proscribed in Buddhist texts. As Dr. Smith explains:

> "While Westerners and some Buddhist scholars may separate out pure Buddhism from the influence of these other religions, *folk Buddhists would see the syncretistic mix merely as facets of the*

10. Smith, *A Christian's Pocket Guide to Buddhism*, 37.

Buddhist religion. Consequently, there is incongruity between orthodox Buddhism and the many varieties of popular Buddhism seen throughout the world today."[11]

Paradoxically though, even in the traditional form of Thai Buddhism that I was ordained into you can see this eclectic tendency at work, albeit to a much lesser extent. Some practices such as worship of spirits in spirit houses, as is common in Thailand, were clearly taught against, but such things as worship of Hindu gods, practicing yoga, homeopathy, and acupuncture were embraced by some of the monks and nuns.

But how did Buddhism travel from Asia to the West? Only a hundred and fifty years ago, it was little known in Europe or the United States. Christianity—the predominant religion in the West for centuries—was bedded deep in the foundations of the nations and their people's lives. Here is a tiny snapshot of how it came.

Early European settlers in North America had virtually no knowledge of Buddhism, but immigrants from China who went there from as early as 1820 soon began building Chinese temples and most of these included Buddhist elements.

British workers were exposed to Buddhism in the former colonies. For example, T. W. Rhys Davids, a civil servant posted to Ceylon, formed the Pali Text Society in 1881 and translated Theravāda Buddhist texts into English, promoting the study of Buddhism.

As knowledge of Buddhism filtered through to the West, some intellectuals became fascinated by it. In 1875 the Theosophical Society, dedicated to the study of the occult and influenced by Buddhist and Hindu beliefs, was formed in New York City. In 1924 the Buddhist Society was founded by Christmas Humphreys in London.

The exodus of thousands of Tibetans in 1959 brought the Dalai Lama and many Tibetan monks to the West. As Eastern religions were popularized in 1960s Britain, it led to the establishment of new Buddhist groups.

People from Asian Buddhist countries continued to migrate to the West, bringing various Buddhist traditions with them.

Meanwhile, as long-distance travel became easier, especially from the 1970s onwards, many westerners were drawn to the East, some of them on a spiritual search. In some Buddhist countries, various Buddhist temples and organizations began to cater for these travellers by arranging English speaking retreats and teachings for them.

11. Ibid., 9, emphasis mine.

More recently, the popularization of Buddhism has been aided by the interest given it by some prominent media figures such as pop stars and Hollywood actors.

In the West we now find many different expressions of Buddhism also. From longstanding traditions from the East to forms of Buddhism with a more Western face, incorporating ideas from Western philosophy, psychotherapy, and art, such as the community my friend David was involved in.

Buddhism, as we have seen, is the philosophy of a man, of which the Apostle Paul warns us of in Scripture:

"Beware lest anyone cheat you through philosophy and empty deceit, according to the tradition of men, according to the basic principles of the world, and not according to Christ" (Col 2:8 nkjv).

You may wonder, then, how do Buddhists come to Christ.

God works in many various ways. Whether for David sensing Jesus calling him to "come back," me having my strong Buddhist belief demolished through watching a Christian video, or a Thai person I heard of who felt God speaking to them through the book of Revelation in Scripture, there seem to be as many ways of coming to know Jesus as there are Buddhists becoming Christians!

One key thing you can do though if you have a Buddhist relative or friend is to begin to pray for them. I didn't know it at the time, but an Anglican nun and a Christian friend of hers were praying for me when I was a Buddhist nun. I'm sure this was instrumental in my eventually coming to Christ. Here is a suggestion of a simple prayer you may like to use:

> *Dear Lord Jesus, I thank you for my friend, [name]. Thank you that you love them so much and long to draw them to yourself. I pray that you will begin to work in them by your Holy Spirit, so that they can see who you truly are and be able to bow their knee to you. In Jesus' name I pray. Amen.*

Please be prepared for the long haul with some Buddhists though—it can take time!

After this brief overview of Buddhism and considering why some westerners may be drawn to it, let's take a look now at the goal of Buddhism. What exactly is nirvāṇa and how does it compare to the Christian goal?

Chapter 2

Nirvāṇa and God

"I am the truth." (Words of Jesus, John 14:6)

Some time ago, I was in a taxi in Bangkok, chatting to the driver to pass the time as we crept along in one of the city's frequent traffic jams. He was Thai and Buddhist, and had pictures of Buddhist monks and symbols strategically placed above his head—a common sight in the taxis of Thailand.

He asked me what I did, so I told him that I work in the church. He responded predictably with the same words I've heard from many Buddhists all over Thailand: "Oh, all religions are good, aren't they?"

He was expecting me just to say "Yes," affirming him in his social politeness and superficial spirituality; but I found I was unable to do so.

I was tired by now of this typical response—of adulating, almost deifying goodness—and was looking to go deeper than this, and if possible, I wanted to take this man with me!

I had a quick think and a prayer and then replied: "Goodness is one thing, but what is more important is truth."

He thought quietly for a long time, until I was beginning to wonder if he would ever speak to me again. Had I offended him? Would he ask me to get out of the taxi? Eventually, to my relief, his inner thoughts were revealed. He simply said: "I have never thought that far."

Actually, on reflection it's an easy option just to focus on "goodness," because most people can be good in some way. Even a gang member who commits murder can be good to his mother! Focusing on the goodness that is within a person or an ideology is a kind gesture but it's certainly not enough. Goodness alone does not necessarily indicate morality or truth. In fact, a "cloak of goodness" can hide debilitating, even paralyzing sins and wickedness in both individuals and societies that are not named, renounced, or dealt with—giving a superficial sense of virtue and truth even if in reality they are not there at all.

Many Thais may like to say, "All religions are good, aren't they?" but I have never heard even one of them say: "All religions are true, aren't they?"

The search for truth is something that has captivated many people down the ages. When I am asked what I have been looking for on my spiritual journey, I can honestly say that it has primarily been a deep desire and quest for truth.

So, what is truth?

The nature of absolute truth is that it is an unalterable and permanent fact: something that *really is*, that *actually exists*, and there is *only one*, not many. This is different from the concept of relative truth, where anything can be considered to be true. An example of this is the way I used to think as a young adult: "That may be true for you, but it's not true for me!"

These days, there is so much on offer that it can be very confusing. So many religious groups and cults claim to have the truth. Certainly, Buddhism and Christianity do, but each teaching that it is something completely different.

Among all the various options, how do we know which is the absolute truth? We need great discernment, for what in the end is a very personal journey of discovery. It isn't easy—just because counterfeit banknotes look and feel real doesn't make them any more valid!

With regard to this important question, let's take a brief look at the Buddhist and Christian goals and their understandings of truth.

Rahula quoting the Buddha:

> "the Absolute Noble Truth (*paramaṃ ariyasaccaṃ*) is Nibbāna, which is Reality."[1]

The Buddhist goal is known by many names, depending on the country and the particular Buddhist tradition. For instance: Nirvāṇa (Sanskrit),

---

1. Rahula, op. cit., 39.

Nibbāna (Pali), shunyata (Sanskrit, in the Mahāyāna tradition), and "enlightenment" in English.

But what is nirvāṇa? It is not easy to define. Even Buddhist monks and scholars can find it hard to explain! This is not surprising, perhaps, as it is considered to be "beyond logic and reasoning."[2]

There are many attempts at describing it though. The Buddha spoke of it as "the unborn, and unconditioned."[3] It is also referred to as the "Absence of desire," and "Cessation."[4]

In the original Pali texts, Musīla, a disciple of the Buddha, is recorded as saying: "The cessation of Continuity and becoming (*Bhavanirodha*) is Nibbāna."[5]

Buddha taught that it is realizable in this life—a state of peace that is realized through giving up all personal desires. One, having done this, he called an Arahant. After death, the Buddha or an Arahant is described as being: "'fully extinct,' because the Buddha or an Arahant has no re-existence after his death."[6]

So, to summarize: Buddha's goal for this life and beyond was to be in a state of absence of desire, craving, and attachment, where, he believed, all becoming ceases. He taught that this is the way to escape suffering in this life and to avoid being reborn.

Recently, I was sharing my story of how I came to Christ in a Buddhist temple at an Anglican women's breakfast in the east of England. When I told them about the Buddhist goal nirvāṇa as described in the Buddhist texts above, they were surprised—like most people in the West that I've shared this with. Often, I find that nirvāṇa is misunderstood here as being some kind of paradise or bliss. This is not so. Buddha's goal was that no one or nothing is born, so that there is no possibility of any sensation of bliss or happiness, as there is simply no one there to experience it. The Buddhist texts acknowledge this, (i.e., as recorded in the discussion between the Buddha's disciple Sāriputta and Udāyi in *What the Buddha Taught*).[7]

2. Ibid., 43.
3. Ibid., 37.
4. Ibid., 36.
5. Ibid., 37.
6. Ibid., 41.
7. Rahula, op. cit., 43.

One of the women at the breakfast made an insightful comment: "It sounds to me like Buddha was after the ultimate escape!" In light of Buddha's spiritual quest to realize the complete end of suffering, I would say she was bang on target.

For years I was completely sold on the teachings and promises of the Buddha, nirvāṇa was my goal. I believed in it enough to give up nearly everything and ordain as a Buddhist nun. It was not until I was close to disrobing (leave the monastic life), after more than thirteen years as a Buddhist, that I seriously questioned it. Now, I see it in a very different light.

In 2006, we had a wonderful seminar at the Bangkok Bible College when our American friend college Professor Dr. Carla Waterman came and taught Thai church leaders and Bible students on "Living in Christ and Growing in Faith, Hope, and Love." At one point, she was teaching on "Hope and Its Opposite" and explaining what happens when we cease to care about those things that really matter, when she read this amazing quote on sloth by Dorothy L. Sayers:

> "[Sloth] is the sin which believes in nothing, cares for nothing, seeks to know nothing, interferes with nothing, enjoys nothing, loves nothing, hates nothing, finds purpose in nothing, lives for nothing, and remains alive only because there is nothing it would die for."[8]

The response was quite extraordinary. As soon as she had finished the quote, two of our most respected senior Thai Pastors, who were sitting together near the front, called out: "That is the Buddhist goal nibbāna! That is the Buddhist goal nibbāna!"

Immediately a tremendous buzz of excitement filled the room.

In her own words, this is what happened to Dr. Waterman at that moment:

> "As I finished reading the Sayers quote, I felt as though I had been hit with a wave of something very dark that was trying to knock me off my feet. At the same time a voice in my ear was saying, 'How dare you proclaim Christian hope in the physical heart of Buddhism!'"

At that point, Dr. Waterman looked at me. I knew that she had touched on something really profound and could see that she was struggling. So, I

8. Sayers, "The Other Six Deadly Sins," 103.

dashed around the room asking our intercessors to pray for her. Quite unwittingly, she had just exposed nirvāṇa in the light of Christ for us all to see! Later, she told me: "It was a powerful, sobering, and triumphant moment all at the same time!"

Actually, she could almost have been quoting from the Buddhist texts themselves describing one having realized nirvāṇa: "He gains nothing, accumulates nothing, not even anything spiritual, because he is free from the illusion of Self, and the 'thirst' for becoming."[9]

It's hard to imagine now that I once could have thought this way, but for some years as a Buddhist nun I would try to convince Christians that nirvāṇa and God were the same. It made sense to me at the time! Some Buddhists like to think this way, "interpreting" God through their Buddhist mindset.

Paradoxically, in his teachings, Buddha did not deny the existence of God, but equally, he did not acknowledge him in any way. So, some Buddhists try to convince open-minded, well-meaning Christians that as God is not clearly denied in Buddhism there can be a place for him, as I did.

What I *deliberately* omitted to tell Christians, however, was that in the practice and outworkings of Buddhism there is absolutely no acknowledgement or true knowledge of God at all. I was merely equating my understanding of nirvāṇa with God.

I used to alarm some Greek Orthodox nuns at interfaith meetings when I expounded these ideas to them. The sad fact is that at the time I really did not know the difference.

Some Buddhist monastics may know *about* God, may even have studied (Christian) theology and are be able to quote Scripture, but I can't see how they could know God personally and remain in Buddhist robes. If they did come to know God, they would have to disrobe, seeing their Buddhist practices as clearly idolatrous having nothing to do with God.

In not knowing God personally, I would go so far as to say that Buddhists don't actually have the relationship or terminology with which to speak of him. It would be like me trying to talk about a particular man, "John Brian Miller," living in Glasgow, Scotland, whom I have never met—where would I start? Interestingly, Pharaoh had the same problem when

---

9. Rahula, op. cit., 43.

talking to Moses: "Who is the Lord, that I should obey His voice?" (Exod 5:2a nkjv).

Elke, a German woman who came out of a New Age background in which she embraced some Buddhist ideas, now ministers with her Dutch husband Martin and describes the moment she could first *see* the reality of God:

> "I realized that I had always behaved as I thought best, or did what was most convenient for me. I had thought I was in contact with God through all sorts of means—meditation, rituals, breathing techniques, special ways of behaving and living, relationships, and many other things. I now suddenly realized that all this time I had been living apart from God, always concentrating on my own interests, wishes and desires. Everything was focused on *me*. I had made myself, and certainly not Him, the centre of my life. In a fraction of a second I realized that my biggest sin had been living without God. I was shocked! . . . I expressed out loud my desire to live for Jesus from that moment on."[10]

So, let's take a quick look at the Christian understanding of truth—bearing in mind that there can be only one absolute truth.

The very first verse in the Bible says: "In the beginning God" (Gen 1:1). Here we see clearly that God is. Later we read that he is a Triune God, meaning three in one: God the Father, God the Son, and God the Holy Spirit.

God reveals himself to us; whether in our day such as we saw in David's story in chapter 1, or to the many people in the past that we read of throughout Scripture. For instance, when God called to Moses from the midst of the burning bush and said: "I am the God of your father, the God of Abraham, the God of Isaac, and the God of Jacob" (Exod 3:6a, also see 6:2).

And he spoke to the people of Israel through the prophet Jeremiah saying: "The Lord is the true God; He is the living God and the everlasting King" (Jer 10:10 nkjv).

Jesus is "the one and only Son, who came from the Father, full of grace and truth" (John 1:14).

---

10. Kamphuis, *Ich war Buddhist*, 147.

He said: "I am the way and the truth and the life. No one comes to the Father except through me" (John 14:6, see also Acts 4:12).

Jesus himself is the way and the truth. It is not that he will point to it; he *is* it.

He came into the world "to testify to the truth" (John 18:37) and to mediate it (John 1:17). He said we shall know the truth—it is knowable—and "the truth will set you free" (John 8:32, 36).

The Holy Spirit is "the Spirit of truth," who "will guide you into all the truth" (John 16:13).

God's Word is truth, by which we need to be sanctified (John 17:17). It is constant, unchanging. Jesus said: "Heaven and earth will pass away, but my words will never pass away" (Matt 24:35).

Significantly, God the Father clearly offers us eternal life, not eternal extinction.

God so loved the world (John 3:16) that he sent his Son, Jesus, to die on a cross. Jesus rose from the dead. He is not "fully extinct" or "unborn" but is alive forever. He is the power of indestructible life and has made a way for us to be with him:

> "Now this is eternal life: that they know you, the only true God,
> and Jesus Christ, whom you have sent." (John 17:3)

"God has given us eternal life, and this life is in his Son. Whoever has the Son has life; whoever does not have the Son of God does not have life." (1 John 5:11b–12)

> "Our Savior, Christ Jesus . . . has destroyed death and has brought
> life and immortality to light through the gospel." (2 Tim 1:10b)

As Oswald Chambers, 1874–1917, an incredibly insightful man of God, said: "Eternal life is not a gift from God, eternal life is the gift of God."[11]

Here then, is the true cessation of suffering: eternally being in the presence of a holy, loving God, along with believers "from every nation, tribe, people and language" (Rev 7:9). It is the ultimate security of never being separated from God again, with no sin or darkness ever able to come in and threaten our relationship with him (see Rev 21:3–4). The very reason we

---

11. Chambers, *My Utmost for His Highest*, April 12.

were born is to come into intimate, godly relationship with our Almighty Creator through Jesus.

Oswald Chambers reminds us:

> "[We exist] to glorify God and to enjoy Him forever."[12]

We see clearly that, while the Buddhist goal is one of "no more becoming," the Christian goal could not be more opposite. For those who believe in Jesus, *the ever more becoming in Christ begins here and goes on throughout eternity.* This is expressed by various saints through the ages:

> "To hearken to the call of the Lord is, as Gregory of Nyssa said centuries ago, to go 'from beginning to beginning, by beginnings that never cease.'"[13]
>
> "Being born again from above is a perennial, perpetual and eternal beginning; a freshness all the time in thinking and in talking and in living, the continual surprise of the life of God."[14]

Whereas Buddhism exalts "non-being" as its goal, God himself is the power, vitality, and source of all being. As it says in Scripture: "You are worthy, our Lord and God, to receive glory and honor and power, for you created all things, and by your will they were created and have their being" (Rev 4:11).

God affirms our being: "For in him we live and move and have our being" (Acts 17:28).

> "The Christian will . . . have an incredible gratefulness to God for the gift of eternal being in Christ, who created all things, and for the opportunity to grow into the fullness of being that He intends for us. To love God and to love truth is never to stop growing in this fullness of being . . . which is eternally ours in Christ."[15]

Although some people may find this hard to relate to, there are those who are attracted to Buddhism, as I was years ago, who at times experience

---

12. Chambers, *Still Higher for His Highest*, January 3. (This is taken from the Westminster Shorter Catechism written by theologians in the 1640s.)

13. Payne, *Heaven's Calling*, 9.

14. Chambers, *My Utmost for His Highest*, January 20.

15. Payne, *Heaven's Calling*, 276.

the feeling of not really knowing who they are, and/or have deep-seated feelings of emptiness. To those people, Buddhism with its doctrine of "no self" and its goal of emptiness often feels natural and familiar.

Leanne Payne, however, identifies such feelings as "having a lack of sense of being." She speaks of it not as a natural state or the truth of how things are at all but as an aspect of our broken humanity. Often this is related to a lack of significant bonding and a failure to come to a secure sense of being in our mother's love (or that of a substitute mother figure) in early life. It is recognized that, especially for children up to the age of five, healthy bonding with and attachment to our mothers is crucial to our long term wellbeing. There can be serious consequences in later life for those who do not have this—an inability to bond with others, poor social skills, lack of self-worth, and anxiety to name a few. I would say now, that to be able to identify with "not having a self" and being deeply familiar with feelings of emptiness, is more an indication of a failure to achieve the most basic of developmental steps—something that desperately needs the love and healing power of Jesus.

It's interesting that, contrary to Buddhism's determined focus on detachment and letting go, we see clearly the importance in life—of natural and healthy attachments to family, friends, interests, and so on—to our sense of wellbeing.

Leanne Payne noticed that over the last decade or so of her inner-healing conferences (Pastoral Care Ministry Schools), many of those who attended went specifically for prayer to receive "a sense of being." It's a sad indication, perhaps, of how prevalent the rupture of natural early bonding can be.

I am truly grateful to God for the prayer I have had in this regard, through both Leanne Payne's and Andy Comiskey's ministries (See "Exploring Further 1: Prayer for a Sense of Being" on page 119).

We are not only affirmed by God in our being, but Christ is the fulfillment of our humanity. As Dr. Waterman reminded us in Thailand, truly God created each of us to be magnanimous—an almost forgotten word these days—meaning; the aspiration of the soul to great things. In magnanimity we embrace the implications of the heights to which we have been raised in Christ.

The Apostle Paul is calling the Thessalonians to rise in magnanimity when he writes:

"To this end we always pray for you, that our God may make you worthy of his calling and may fulfill every resolve for good and every work of faith by his power, so that the name of our Lord Jesus may be glorified in you, and you in him, according to the grace of our God and the Lord Jesus Christ." (2 Thess 1:11–13, esv)

Life without God is empty and meaningless—in that respect Buddha was right. The great sadness is, he missed the truth of the existence of God, the source of all being and becoming.

"Only the greatest of the Christian philosopher-theologians can rightly express our struggle between nothingness on the one hand (that dreadful place of estrangement from God and therefore from our eternal selves in Him) and with eternally being and becoming on the other ... Throughout our lives and at every stage of our becoming, though we see as through a glass darkly, if we consistently love and honor truth, we will have the Spirit-given capacity to know it in all its fullness."[16]

After looking at these goals, albeit briefly, I hope it sheds some light for you as to why I consider the Buddhist goal of nirvāṇa to be diametrically opposed to knowing God and spending eternity with him. (See "Exploring Further 15: Some Important Differences between Nirvāṇa and Eternal Life with God" on page 145).

How does this help us in understanding and reaching our Buddhist friends?

It is very important when witnessing to Buddhists to keep in mind that they have no true understanding of who God is, even if they try and convince you that they do. If you are not sure or clear about this as you witness to Buddhists, you will be wading through confusion and getting lost following bunny trails!

I hope the following story will help to illustrate this.

Not long after I became a Christian, I was having lunch with a Thai Buddhist friend who is a sincere spiritual seeker. She had known me as a Buddhist nun and was interested to know why I had disrobed.

As I was talking to her and sharing about God, I could see that she had no idea who or what I was talking about (see 2 Cor 4:4). So, I prayed

16. Ibid., 21–22.

quietly, asking God to help me to explain him to her. He gave me a picture of a desert and a banqueting table. The desert had nothing in it: it was a lifeless, lonely, dangerous place, which to me spoke of Buddhism. The banqueting table was a picture of life and blessings, with many people sitting around it enjoying each other's company as they partook of the delicious fare together. To me, it described Christianity.

I shared these two pictures with my friend. Interestingly, I could see that it was really hard and challenging for her to think of the picture of life and plenty as a desirable one. She was so trained in focusing on emptiness and nothingness as her goal, that she was "naturally" more attracted to the desert!

She let me pray for her that God would give her understanding, and I trust that in his time he will. Into the desolation of the unborn Buddhist nothingness, we paint pictures of our living hope in Christ.

As you pray (with other Christians or alone) for your Buddhist friend, a prayer along these lines as God leads would be helpful:

> *Dear Lord Jesus, please help my friend [name] to be able to discern the truth. Where they have believed that emptiness, non-being, nirvāṇa, is superior to knowing you, please help them see it clearly for the paralyzing reality it actually is. We pray that its hold on them will be loosened. Please touch their mind and cause them to doubt. Free their mind, we pray, in Jesus' name. Amen.*

To conclude, Martin Kamphuis (the husband of Elke quoted previously and a Dutchman who for many years was seriously involved in Tibetan Buddhism and New Age practices), explains how he felt as a young Christian, when at times his mind drifted back to Buddhism:

> "Sometimes I thought to myself, 'Perhaps it *is* right in some ways. Its peaceful attitude towards all living things is exemplary. Many Christians could learn a thing or two from Buddhism.'
>
> "Whenever I harboured such thoughts, an indefinable emptiness would creep into my heart for days, leaving me very passive, especially with regard to praying and reading the Bible. I was able to unmask this emptiness only when I realised that I had been flirting with Buddhist teaching. I would immediately ask God for forgiveness, and the inner emptiness would melt away like snow in the sunshine.

"... As soon as I accepted even parts of Buddhist teaching again—though they might seem good from a human point of view—I was committing myself once more to the whole spiritual structure.

"Only now did I recognize the real face of Buddhism. Its peacefulness and its moral standards appear initially very attractive, but it turns out to be a subtle spirit that wants to take me over and drag me down into the terrible, lonely emptiness of Nirvāṇa, where there is no relationship with a personal God, and where there is no life.

"Now I *knew*: I had to distance myself from Buddhism completely if I were to keep on experiencing the fullness of Jesus Christ, his love and his forgiveness."[17]

With this in mind, let's now take a closer look at how Buddhism functions: the role of meditation (including "mindfulness") in realizing nirvāṇa, and how Buddhist meditation differs from Christian prayer.

17. Kamphuis, op. cit., 193–194.

Chapter 3

Meditation and Prayer

"I am the life." (Words of Jesus, John 14:6)

Not long after becoming a Christian, I met with a good friend of mine, a Dutch Buddhist woman who was the mother of one of the monks. We had known each other for some time, having met in the temple where she often came to visit her son. I was eager to see her again and to share about my newfound Christian faith with her.

After we had coffee together, I started to tell her why I had become a Christian. Talking to her this time, however, felt very odd. Usually we communicated very well, but now it was as if we were talking in different languages. Although we were both speaking English, we simply could not understand each other!

To be honest, it wasn't a good meeting and later, when she had left, I prayed asking God what was going on. What was blocking me from sharing about Jesus with her? It was then that he gave me a "picture"—a mental image given in prayer, which, when discerned that it really is of God, is one way that he communicates with his people—of a thick metal band, like an enormous ring, around her mind which was stopping her from being able to hear or understand me.

Shortly after, not knowing what it meant, I shared this picture with my vicar's wife, who is experienced in prayer. Her response was: "That's important, a key to understanding the situation. Pray into it." So I did, and it then became clear to me that the picture was speaking of Buddhism being a stronghold around the mind—like having a helmet over your head. Not one that protects, but one that keeps the truth of the gospel out. It occurred to me, *That's why when I was a Buddhist I couldn't understand Christians when they shared with me about Jesus.* What they said would bypass my mind—like water off a duck's back, it couldn't take hold. I simply couldn't "see" this Jesus; I couldn't understand why they kept going on about him, and usually I felt very irritated when they did!

I found a Scripture to explain it:

> "Even if our gospel is veiled, it is veiled to those who are perishing, whose minds the god of this age has blinded, who do not believe, lest the light of the gospel of the glory of Christ, who is the image of God, should shine on them." (2 Cor 4:3–4 nkjv)

This understanding, given to me in those early days, has played a key role in my prayers and approach to evangelizing Buddhists over the years since.

With this in mind, let's have a look at how the Buddha endeavored to "realize" nirvāṇa.

There were several factors involved in his path, but meditation played a key role. To this day, in most Buddhist traditions, meditation of various kinds takes a significant place in the life of any serious Buddhist practitioner.

Of the different types that Buddha practiced, a significant one is insight meditation—an analytical method based on mindfulness and awareness. (It is aspects of this type of Buddhist meditation, and especially mindfulness, that has found its way into mainstream psychology directly from Theravāda Buddhism.) This type of meditation practice forms the basis of Theravāda Buddhist monastic life. Monks and nuns give much of their time and energy to it, as I did for about eight years.

The Buddhist practitioner is taught to develop awareness in the present moment of the arising and ceasing of phenomena such as body, feelings, sensations, ideas, and to observe them with detachment—dispassionately, as a scientist observes some object—not judging, not attaching to anything, inclining toward the emptiness of mind, rather than the conditions.

This type of Buddhist meditation aims at detachment from *all* the content of our minds. For example, if I had the thought, *I like the color blue*, as a Buddhist I was trained to see it as just a passing thought and not belonging to me (or "a self"). Now as a Christian, I see that thought as part of me, an expression of my character. I may, of course, change my mind in ten years time and prefer red to blue, but it would still be me thinking that thought. Just because it had changed doesn't prove that the thought was empty or that I don't have a self.

I think it is important to note that mindfulness and awareness of themselves and outside the context of Buddhism are natural human qualities—abilities of the mind to be attentive and observant, bringing presence of mind. They are useful and much needed in everyday life. However, for the serious Buddhist practitioner the use of mindfulness and awareness in the context of Buddhist insight meditation truly becomes something else.

I see it like this. If you think of an individual as being like a tree:

> the roots represent our being,
> the trunk represents our individuality,
> the branches represent the expression of various aspects of our humanity such as our personality, character, and gifts,
> the leaves represent our feelings, emotions, thoughts and so on.

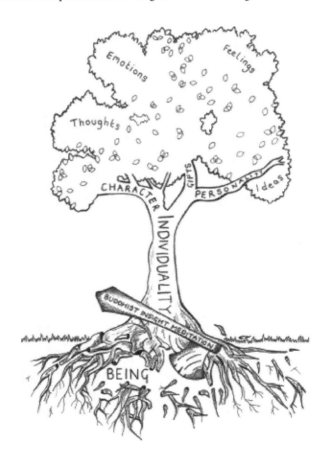

The Buddhist goal is to have no more tree, that it becomes *extinct*—no more becoming, nirvāṇa. In attempting to realize this, as we see in the tree illustration, an axe chops at the *roots* of the tree. In order to make sure that you kill a tree, you need to destroy it at its roots, not merely chop it down at its trunk. This to me, represents the sharp and powerful tool of Buddhist insight meditation, a key part of which is mindfulness.

However, mindfulness is being used here very differently from how it would function naturally. Here it focuses in, bringing awareness "microscopically"—thought by thought, feeling by feeling, and sensation by sensation—of the arising and ceasing of all phenomena, *and*, at the same time, all the phenomena it becomes aware of is being viewed through a mind already conditioned through the acceptance of Buddha's teaching—to believe that everything is impermanent, unsatisfactory, and not belonging to a self, and that any volitional actions will create the propensity for existence (karma). It is belief in these teachings, then, that gives rise to the strong determination in the Buddhist practitioner to let go—not attach to but merely observe—*any* conditions of mind or body it becomes aware of in an ongoing way. And, like when using an axe, the practitioner's committed determination to meditate works gradually but persistently.

Thus, as used in this type of Buddhist meditation, mindfulness drifts far from its natural and blessed function. In combination with the Buddha's teachings, it becomes a significant constituent part of a powerfully destructive tool, "sharpened" to chop away at our sense of self. The final aim, when the axe has cut through the roots of the tree, is the cessation of the attachment and desire to be or to exist itself: nirvāṇa, the Buddhist goal.

When Buddha concluded that to exist in any form was suffering, from which he wanted to be free (nirvāṇa), I would say that in effect he "struck a death blow" to being—the very desire to exist. This he labeled as ultimate truth.

I'm not saying that the he encouraged suicide in any way, as he certainly didn't, but it was clear that his goal was to not be attached to this life or to become in any sense.

I remember my mother and father coming to visit me one time when I was a nun in the temple. My dad was a very down to earth kind of man who spoke his mind. Neither he nor my mom could make *any* sense of Buddhism, though they had tried for years. It was hard for them to come to terms with the skinny, distant person I had become. At the time of this visit, I was deeply into Buddhist mindfulness meditation and the practice of letting go.

As usual, Mom had baked lots of cakes and brought heaps of food for me. It's only in retrospect that I realize how deeply concerned she was for me and how significant a role she played in helping me survive through those ascetic years.

After lunch, I was trying hard to find things to chat with them about, but as the nuns didn't watch television, listen to the radio, receive newspapers, and spent much of the time trying to "detach" from the world, I wasn't exactly full of topics of conversation, even though I'm quite chatty by nature.

Suddenly, I had an inspiration: "I know, I'll ask dad about football." (Our family home was behind the town's football ground.) So, trying to sound interested, I asked: "Dad, how's our football team doing this year?"

He replied shocked at how out of touch I was. "It's summer!" he said, "They don't play in summer." Then he added: "Oh dear, if ever you leave this place you'll have to take a course on how to be normal again!"

Actually, there was some truth in his words, as I was to discover later when I did disrobe.

Persisting in intensive meditation of this sort does, over time, have a powerful effect on you, I would say. Gradually, it takes you to a dormant twilight as you grow increasingly detached, in a sense paralyzed, by choosing to disengage from life rather than lay hold of it. Souls which are meant to live shrink, growing passive and distant. The practitioners aspire and encourage each other on toward the hope, not of fulfillment, but rather of nothingness and emptiness.

Charles Williams, the Christian author and friend of C. S. Lewis, described such a goal I feel, but from a Christian viewpoint:

"Hell . . . is an image of an unchanging state which endures no more *becoming*, and to dwell in the alienated self is to dwell in hell."[1]

Usually, by this stage of deep commitment, Buddhism has bound your mind so tightly that it is virtually impossible to seriously think outside its confines. It's almost as if it's designed to imprison you from being able to come to a true knowledge of God.

1. From *Descent into Hell* (Wm B Eerdmans Publishing Co, 1937), quoted by Leanne Payne in *Real Presence*, 154.

For me, it was a tremendous battle to get out of Buddhism—particularly over my mind.

Even after God in his mercy touched me as a Buddhist nun, I was so accustomed and committed through intensive meditation practice to letting go that I tried to "let go" of God himself! But, despite my resistance and rebellion, mercifully, he did not give up on me.

So, how was I released from it? In my early days of being a Christian, when Jackie Pullinger (an exemplary Christian based in Hong Kong) prayed for me, she thanked God that he had "bypassed my mind and touched my spirit." Her words were instrumental in helping me understand and articulate what had happened to me.

Buddhism, denying that we have a soul and a spirit, aims to escape suffering predominantly through the mind; by means of meditation, analysis, teaching, and so on. And, as we have seen, its strong grip had been on my mind. But God had touched my spirit by his Holy Spirit, and his life was born in me. That's the meaning of being a Christian: being alive in our spirits: "the Spirit gives birth to spirit" (John 3:6).

That's why I could now see God was real, having previously denied him fervently—and, knowing God was real, I was able to stop trying to dismiss him through my mind. It was not long after this that my longstanding faith in Buddhism was to collapse completely.

Jackie's prayer showed me that the awakening to the truth of the reality of God was in my spirit, not in my mind. But, once alive in my spirit, truth began to be processed and understood in my mind (Rom 8:6)—and so the journey of discipleship began.

This understanding proved a great help to me in explaining the picture of the thick metal band around my Buddhist friend's mind I mentioned at the beginning of the chapter.

Buddha described the way, he claimed, that led to the cessation of suffering as a "middle path" (I explained this briefly in chapter 1, on page 8). Having practiced it for around eight years, though, I would say it definitely leans toward asceticism, making it more of an extreme path, rather than a moderate one which its name suggests. Our lives in the temple of meditation and sensory deprivation—such as limited food and sleep leading to my weakened health—stood witness to that. I would say that the "middle path" is more an ideal of moderation rather than a reality.

Some time back, a missionary friend, Yvonne, and I were praying together for some Thai Buddhist friends—lay people—in Bangkok. As we prayed, Yvonne had a picture of one of them being wrapped in grave clothes like Lazarus in John 11:1–44, unable to move or get out of the confines of Buddhism. However, Jesus, out of his love and compassion for her, was calling her out into life and being.

As we continued to pray, we "saw" the many layers of tightly wound bandages start to come off. We caught a glimpse of her face as it started to peek through. Then her arms began moving, trying to get out, then her legs. Eventually, even her heart was freed to become a heart of flesh, and her mind released from its strong pull toward emptiness.

She had spent her life binding herself up in these grave clothes, but now she was freed from the grip of death for life.

This was a very encouraging and helpful prayer time for us!

Thinking about it, the confines of Buddhist monastic discipline, with its many rules (227 for monks) covering practically every aspect of life including deportment, and the use of requisites such as robes and bowl, could easily be likened to grave clothes. The Buddhist robe itself as used in public, is designed to be confining, so that you can't swing your arms about, move energetically, or run in public.

For the serious practitioner, there is also a clear focus in Buddha's teachings on the contemplation of death. For example he advised his monks and nuns to meditate on (by looking at) corpses. I remember, as a nun, being earnestly led around Bangkok by a Thai Buddhist friend to various hospitals in the heat. I had asked her to help me find an autopsy to meditate on, but—on reflection, most thankfully!—we didn't succeed.

Let's take a look at some of the practical outworkings of Buddhist meditation in everyday life. We'll start in a Thai supermarket.

About five years ago in Bangkok on an early Saturday morning—I like to do my grocery shopping before the crowds get out—I was on the escalator going up to the Thai Macro store. I was feeling only half awake when a couple of women, in their forties, came and stood close behind me. They were chatting in Thai, and I don't expect they imagined I could understand them.

One of them was sharing about her problems and suffering, while the other was giving her advice: "You have to *pattibat taam* [practice Buddhism and meditate]!" Buddhist meditation is really respected by the Thais and is often used by them for many different reasons, such as to make merit or to calm the mind.

Suddenly, there on the escalator, something important dawned on me.

When suffering arises, Buddhists—including those living a family life—are encouraged to withdraw from the world and meditate, developing awareness in order to practice letting go of their thoughts and feelings. I realized that this is really passive: escaping their problems through their minds, through meditation. It may give a feeling of more distance and detachment for a while, but the *actual problem* is often not dealt with (directly or sufficiently) and can remain unresolved.

I can clearly see this occurring in my past with, for instance, some significant painful emotional issues. After many years of Buddhist meditation and monastic discipline, I found these practices had served more to put a temporary lid on my feelings and emotions, containing them and keeping them "on hold," than experiencing real change or healing. As a Christian, I have needed much healing prayer over the years before I could experience any significant healing and inner freedom.

As I look back, remembering how earnest I was in Buddhist meditation and the practice of mindfulness and how much I gave up for it, I have to conclude, if I'm honest, that I really don't see any point to it now. To try and let go of yourself and the world through mindfulness and awareness really doesn't make much sense. I can't see that our minds, or our humanity, were designed for this. However much I tried to let go of myself, the simple fact is: I am! We are all an intrinsic part of this world and there is a higher purpose in that. Finding our place in it and learning to engage with life appropriately is, I would say, far more relevant and purposeful than trying to use the mind to just be aware and let it all go.

Buddha was undoubtedly sincere in his search, but I see in Buddhism and its goal a profound lack of understanding and acceptance of who we truly are in our totality, and as a result it has a powerfully destructive attack on our selves and beings. This imbalance, I would say, is much exacerbated by its overdependence on the use of the rational and analytical aspects of the mind: a process in which Buddhist meditation plays a major part, serving to silence and dismiss with all it can muster, the reality and voice of our true selves, hearts, and spirits.

Buddhism conjures a harmless picture, with its emphasis on tolerance, compassion, peacefulness, and mindfulness. But Buddha, by missing completely the existence of God, joined the pagan (in the original sense of the word) world. By mere human effort he sought knowledge and understanding outside of God, and carefully spun an illusion: the way of apparent godliness for the "God-less." His monks and nuns dutifully observe their discipline, but by misperceiving voluntary incarceration as liberation, they mindfully, and with great persistence, tread the well worn path toward an empty chasm of non-being and extinction that Buddha directed them to.

"Mindfulness" these days is being practiced widely outside of Buddhists temples also. Reports of the use of it are so common at the moment that it has reached the national newspapers quite often. For instance; it is being used in mainstream psychology (such as in Mindfulness-Based Cognitive Therapy, MBCT, and Mindfulness-Based Stress Reduction, MBSR), and also in "mindfulness meditation" which is popular for use in "relaxation," and is widely available digitally, through various apps. Some of my friends have mentioned it in other contexts, too—one works in a hospice where a colleague would like to introduce it into the "breathlessness clinics" they hold, while another, a missionary, heard about it on her Christian counseling course.

Christian friends have asked me what I think about it.

To be honest, I am concerned about its use because of the subversive influence of Buddhism. It's important, I feel, to be aware of its source; for instance, I've heard that the obvious Buddhist roots of mindfulness meditation within current psychotherapy tend to be downplayed. And, as I mentioned in my explanation of the metaphor of the tree, mindfulness, in the context of Buddhist meditation, drifts far from its natural function. Also, it is not uncommon for some of these therapies and popular meditation practices using mindfulness to be steeped in Buddhist thought and doctrine, although often it is not identified as such. For example, in some therapies the clients are taught that "they are not their thoughts," which actually trains them in the Buddhist understanding of "non-self" and emptiness.

The powerful side-effects when people—including Christians—yield themselves to these various techniques stem from Buddhism's quiet and unobtrusive ability to change completely someone's view of themselves and of reality—which I consider to be a serious matter. Many of those who are drawn to these techniques would simply not be able to recognize the Buddhist elements, let alone the nature of the goal that it is (subliminally) pointing them toward.

I'm sometimes asked if I think it's alright for Christians to practice Buddhist meditation since it aims to calm and still the mind. My response is always the same: I do not think that it is.

To explain this, I pick up an object, i.e. a Bible, hold it up and say:
"The foundation of Christianity is God."

Then I put it down and look toward the place where the Bible was and say:
"The foundation of Buddhism is not God."

So, Buddhism and Christianity are foundationally and fundamentally different. They belong to different kingdoms (Col 1:13).

This understanding is crucial when relating to Buddhists.

The Bible speaks of only two spiritual kingdoms:

the kingdom of God, of light (Matt 3:2),

and the kingdom of God's enemy, of darkness (Eph 2:2).

There is no mention of a bridge between these two kingdoms, where citizens from each can meet and mingle happily together. Some Christians assume a neutral "middle ground" that scripturally is not there at all. Actually, at times when the two kingdoms do meet, it can be explosive. For instance, the intense confusion and "battle" over my mind that I experienced after God had touched me in the temple (see chapter 6 on the illusory nature of evil) I would say was a result of the meeting of the two kingdoms!

It is because of where its foundations lie that I say it is not appropriate for Christians to practice *any* form of Buddhist meditation (mindfulness or otherwise), or to incorporate any aspect of Buddhism into their Christian lives, however helpful it may appear from the outside. *It is not actually possible to separate the experience of (aspects of) Buddhism out from its spiritual roots at a deeper level, there is a link.* Sorry to use this illustration, but it's a bit like trying to look at pornography impartially, we can't, and it will have an effect. We need to keep our allegiance to Christ clear and depart from the notion that as believers we can remain spiritually neutral regarding such things.

Christianity is rich in its traditions of prayer and contemplation, and there is much to draw on. And all of it will have God the Father, God the Son, and God the Holy Spirit firmly at its center, whereas Buddhism does not. That's the important thing to look for.

Instead of pursuing "detachment" as emphasized in Buddhism, if we "attach" to God—meaning to become close to him and intimate in the most godly sense—our detachment from all that is amiss in our lives will take care of itself!

I sometimes hear it said that Buddhists "pray." This is not actually possible, as in Buddhism there is no one and nothing to pray to. You can't pray to emptiness or a philosophy, whereas Christians pray to God.

As Buddhism is a stronghold around your Buddhist friend's mind and over their thinking, prayer is essential for them. Coming alive in their spirit is essential to their freedom. You may wish to use a prayer like this, either together with Christian friends or alone:

> *Dear Lord Jesus, we come to you to pray for [name]. We ask that you please go ahead by your Holy Spirit and touch their spirit, so that your life is born in them. We pray that where "the god of this age" [2 Cor 4:4] has blinded their mind, you will break the power of the strong band of Buddhism around their mind so that they can be freed and renewed. We ask that the light of the gospel of Christ, who is the image of God, should shine on them. In Jesus' name we pray. Amen.*

Now that we have looked at meditation and prayer, let's consider another important Buddhist concept, karma, in light of God's grace.

Chapter 4

Karma and Grace

"People are destined to die once, and after that to face judgment."
(Heb 9:27)

I sometimes hear people in Britain mention "karma" as they chat with others. "Oh, that's your karma," for example, can casually roll off someone's tongue. Whenever I hear something like this, I think to myself: *Hmm. I wonder if you have any real idea what that means?* Let's take a closer look at this significant Buddhist concept, and then think about it from a Christian viewpoint.

A while ago, in Bangkok, I was watching an episode of a Thai TV chat show following the lives of some foreigners who have settled in Thailand. This program is popular because, unlike in Britain, there are relatively few who truly integrate into Thai society, and local people are fascinated by the stories of those who do.

This particular episode focused on a European businessman who had lived in Thailand for many years and had been very successful. He had a Thai wife who I expect was a folk Buddhist, as most people in the provinces are (approximately 95 percent of Thais are Theravāda Buddhist and around 1 percent are Christian). We saw pictures of a Buddhist ceremony, so this man was obviously sympathetic to Buddhism to some degree. Being compassionate and genuinely moved by the poverty he saw in Thailand, he had established a foundation to help the poor and over the years had initiated many excellent projects such as building schools. It was obvious that he was well respected locally for his hard work and kindness.

During the program his wife was interviewed and was asked how she felt about her husband's many good works helping the poor. I was surprised when the interviewer began by asking: "At first, you didn't agree with the foundation, did you?"

"No," she replied, "I didn't agree with it in the beginning, because as a Thai I'm used to giving only at certain times of the year and on special occasions, not all the time." This attitude stems from the belief that Buddhist customs and traditions provide opportunities to "make merit"—in other words, to do "good actions" in order to try to get a "good rebirth" in the next life. She continued: "I thought, *Why should we help all year?* In the end, though, I saw that we were helping people and that it was a good thing to do."

She got there in the end, but let's take a closer look to see what might have been at the root of her initial reluctance. Let me start by briefly explaining the Buddha's teaching on karma which he adopted out of Hinduism, prevalent in India in his day (the sixth century bc), and which I also believed in for many years.

Buddha taught that karma is its own "law," a theory of cause and effect with no God or higher power sitting in judgment. (This is quite different from the biblical principle that "you reap what you sow": "to the sinful nature destruction, to the Spirit, eternal life" [Gal 6:7b–8].) More specifically, he taught that karma is "volitional action," any action done with intent; "good actions" lead to "making merit and good effects" and "bad actions" lead to "bad effects."

The results of past karma, Buddha taught, will inevitably continue to manifest themselves at some point, either in this life or in the life to come after death through "rebirth" into various "realms" of existence. "Good actions" lead to a good "rebirth," such as a human being or a god, and "bad actions" lead to a bad one, such as being born as an animal or a ghost. Included in the Buddhist "realms" are "heavens and hells," but these are not comparable to the Christian heaven and hell. In Buddhism, no state of existence is considered permanent/eternal, even the heavens and hells.

You may wonder what the "good and bad volitional actions" are. It was Buddha himself who agreed on the definition of them. For example, he said it was a "bad action" to kill *any* living creature, even a rat or a cockroach, as he believed they are all beings caught up in the cycle of birth, death, and rebirth.

In Buddhism, doing "bad volitional actions" is seen to be a personal choice coming from "ignorance," not a violation against a holy God who defines sin for us and to whom we have to answer. *So, "bad volitional actions" are not comparable to the biblical understanding of sin, which does not exist in Buddhism.* To quote Rahula: "there is no 'sin' in Buddhism, as sin is understood in some religions."[1]

In that way, the theory of karma is not so much a "moral code" as the self-reliant practitioner has the freedom to choose whether or not to do "good or bad actions," feeling "free of moral judgment." It's really up to them, as in the end they're the one "paying" for it! The idea of "choice" and having many lives can encourage some to cast off restraint—which can prove very dangerous. This may help to explain, for instance, the high numbers of young men in Thailand who are killed in motorbike accidents after heavy drinking.

Buddha taught that the ending of one life merely conditions the start of another life—and that it is not the same self or soul that gets "reborn," so he didn't speak of a "person" being reborn but of a "being." For example, a being could be born as a man in Colombo, Sri Lanka in one life and as a rat in London, England in the next life with no connection between the two except for "the remaining results of karma."[2]

Buddha claimed that as long as karma (volitional action) is being made, it will result in being caught in the cycle of birth, death, and rebirth in some form or other. As long as there is the "desire" to become, "the cycle of continuity" (*saṃsāra* in Pali) goes on.

In equating *any* form of rebirth or existence with repeated suffering, Buddha's ultimate goal was to make no more karma, to eliminate any "thirst" to exist. This, he said, would result in no more rebirth of any kind—which was his goal.

Certainly as a Buddhist nun that was my goal, too. However, I would say that a typical lay Buddhist—someone living a family life in a Buddhist country, for example—would not be so focused on that, as many would see

---

1. Rahula, op. cit., 3.

2. I am indebted to Paul Williams, Emeritus Professor of Indian and Tibetan Philosophy, University of Bristol for this idea.

it as too high an aspiration for them, but rather on how to secure a "good next life." They may listen to talks on nirvāṇa, or read about it, without any real expectation of trying to realize it.

By concluding that life consists of endless rounds of sorrow and suffering, Buddha taught that the origin of the universe must be (a negative one) "ignorance" (*avijjā*). *That is why God as Creator is often perceived in a negative light by Buddhists.* Buddha believed that there was no first cause possible (as everything is relative and inter-dependent) and that a beginning to the universe could not be perceived.

Karma for a Buddhist is very significant as it is the whole explanation of their existence. It not only explains how they came into being but also gives them an answer to their present state, whether favorable or not.

If you were born into a happy and/or comfortable life and were wealthy, healthy, and well educated, it would be assumed that this was the result of good karma—you must have done a lot of good things in a past life. However, if you were born into a poor family or were really suffering, it would be assumed that you had done bad things in a past life and that suffering was inescapable as a result. In a sense, your difficulties could be regarded as your fault, as you have "shaped" your present circumstances through your past actions and are suffering as a way to "work off" the results of that karma in this life.

Although the theory of karma points to each individual as being "responsible" for their own future through their volitional actions, they can easily become a "victim" of an unseen "past life" if things are not going well for them. (Sadly, it may even blind some people to recognize they are victims of exploitation and injustice.)

Christian author, the late George Appleton, explains it well:

> "The Buddhist idea of karma can tend towards fatalism, hopelessness, self-excusing and pessimism. Buddhism has no possibility of forgiveness; Karma is the iron law to which there is no exception."[3]

So, for the woman in the TV interview and for many lay Buddhists in Thailand, doing acts of goodness may be motivated more by a concern

---

3. Appleton, George, *The Christian Approach to the Buddhist.* London: Edinburgh House Press, 1958, 52. Quoted in Smith, *A Christian's Pocket Guide to Buddhism*, 67.

to "make merit" than by a heartfelt response to needs in a given situation. This can result in "good actions" being quite contrived and measured in approach. It seems, that at first, the woman in the interview honestly could not see the need to help the poor outside of the prescribed times and ways of the Buddhist customs and traditions. Interestingly, her European husband, who no doubt had some Christian influence in his past, felt a genuine compassion for the needy and, much to his credit, responded accordingly. I feel that his response helped his wife to see what true, heartfelt compassion looks like outside of her Buddhist mindset, which had been so shaped by the idea of "making merit" and karma.

What are some of the other "merit-making" activities that Buddhism teaches? It is considered highly meritorious to give gifts to Buddhist temples, monks, and nuns. This explains the great flood of people going to make offerings at temples on certain special Buddhist days and as a result of which, needless to say, many temples have become very wealthy.

As a Buddhist nun, I had direct experience of being on the receiving end of such attempts to make merit. Some Thai Buddhists were extremely generous toward me over a long period of time. Often after their visits I would be piled up with many gifts—delicacies to eat, fine-quality cloth for making robes, and so on. It was amazing! However, when I saw them again as a Christian, I found that their generosity dropped off dramatically. At first, I was a bit perplexed by this; but then I realized that as a Christian and not a Buddhist nun I was no longer a "high-merit target" in their eyes and so there was little reason for them to be as generous toward me.

Another personal experience is the time, as a Christian, I was giving a rice meal to a hungry beggar and his children on the streets of Bangkok. A Thai lady who was watching closely remarked (in Thai): "You're good at making merit!" The implication being that by giving rice to the beggar and his family, I was getting something for *me*.

I took a moment to think then replied: "No, I'm certainly not doing it to 'make merit.' I'm giving them food because God loves them and they need some lunch!"

Let me explain a bit more what I feel might be happening here. From the examples I have given, we see that the way people live out and practice their belief in karma can over time result in an unhealthy separation of their "head" and "heart" responses. In other words, it can create a division between what they believe or think about a situation with how they feel about it and respond to it. For instance, believing (in their rational minds) that someone's situation is simply a result of their past karma has the potential, when taken seriously, to override their emotional responses. This may result in a distortion and/or repression of their God-given feelings such as compassion, kindness, and generosity.

Dr. Alex Smith observes that in the Buddhist context compassion

> "is more an intellectual awareness of that state than of any explicit emotional feeling or attendant action to alleviate the suffering state. . . . Buddhist compassion is not essentially the direct result of emotional feeling or of the call to respond with merciful action."[4]

There are, of course, some Buddhists who do exhibit deep concern for others, and there are notable Buddhist groups and individuals who have established compassionate aid agencies in various parts of the world. However, as Dr. Smith observes:

> "the presence of Buddhist agencies in times of natural disaster is still generally quite minimal compared with that of Christian aid agencies."[5]

So, although Buddhism often appears to be compassionate, what is often not seen (as we have considered above) is the motivation behind some of the "acts of compassion."

Having looked briefly at the Buddhist concept of karma, let's now consider how it is seen from a Christian and biblical viewpoint.

"People are destined to die once, and after that to face judgment" (Heb 9:27). From Scripture, we see that Jesus did not recognize karma in any shape or form, or the idea of being endlessly reborn into various states and realms. The Bible tells us that we have one life only (here on earth), and that it is God himself who will determine where we will go once this life has ended, not the results of our karma or volitional actions. Depending on whether or not we know Jesus and obey God's Word, we will either spend

4. Smith, "Suffering and Compassion in Buddhism and Christianity." In De Neui, *Suffering*, 66.

5. Ibid., 66.

eternity with God or experience eternal separation from him, which the Bible calls hell or everlasting destruction (2 Thess 1:8–9).

There is no recognition of "good and bad volitional actions" as Buddha defined them. Rather, through his Word, God clearly defines what sin is for us. As the Creator of the universe, and completely understanding its "mechanics," moral and otherwise, truly he is the only one in the position to do that. A (mere) human being, with human limitations does not have the capacity for that—however lofty and idealistic their philosophy, it cannot help but paint an incomplete and somewhat misguiding picture.

Where the Bible does mention being "born again"—Jesus said, "No one can see the kingdom of God unless they are born again" (John 3:3)—this is totally different to the Buddhist idea of karma and is not connected or related to it in any way. It refers to when a person is born from above through God's Holy Spirit. We become alive in God and hence children of God (John 1:13).

It's interesting to me how very differently Buddhism and Christianity see "desire." In Buddhism it is taught that *all* types of "desire," "craving," and "thirst" lead to volitional actions both good and bad, which are considered to be the cause of rebirth and "bondage." So, Buddhism teaches that *all desires* need to be let go of. I find the reflections of Professor Russell Bowers, a former missionary to Cambodia, very insightful here:

> "for the Christian not all desire is wrong. The biblical words for desire are used for a variety of longings: good, bad, and indifferent. . . . Desire itself is not our enemy; evil desire is. God himself desires (Ps. 132:13–14); Jesus desires (Luke 22:15); the Spirit desires (Gal. 5:16), and at times grants what people want (Ps. 21:2). Christians are commanded to desire certain things (1 Cor. 12:31). So desire *in se* is not bad. The question for the Christian is, 'What is the source of and cure for the *evil* that prompts evil cravings and their lamentable consequences?' rather than, 'How can we eliminate *all* desire?'"[6]

Unlike Buddhism, the Bible speaks of a beginning. The first verse in the Bible tells us: "In the beginning God created the heavens and the earth" (Gen 1:1). We see that God is the Creator of everything, including all forms

---

6. Bowers, Russell H. Jr., "What You Don't Know Can Hurt You: Ignorance as a Cause of Suffering in Buddhism and Christianity." In De Neui, *Suffering*, 43.

of life—people, animals, fish, birds—and that he delights in everything he has brought into the world: "God saw all that he had made, and it was very good" (Gen 1:31).

The Bible affirms that we have a soul (Matt 16:26; 1 Thess 5:23b). There is nothing written about us being soulless "beings" shaped and propelled by the results of karma in and out of various life forms, struggling to "make merit" for a good rebirth or trying to escape being reborn altogether. Quite the reverse: we see a picture of God's great contentment with all the creatures he has made and a sense that each one has its rightful order, place, and purpose. God has made us intentionally and we have been known by him from the beginning: "For you created my inmost being; you knit me together in my mother's womb" (Ps 139:13).

God has a plan for our lives, and he has already written it. We don't need to struggle to make our future "happen" through our own "merit-making" and "good actions": "All the days ordained for me were written in your book before one of them came to be" (Ps 139:16).

God's plan, will, and purpose for each individual human life are "to give you hope and a future" (Jer 29:11).

Finding God's will for our lives, however, is dependent on us first putting our faith in Jesus Christ and accepting his free gift of salvation. (For more details, please see "Exploring Further 2: The Simple Gospel Message" on page 120.)

As we have seen, for Buddhists who believe in karma, securing a good future is dependent on them and what they do. As Christians, we do have a part to play, but as Scripture shows us, that is founded and built upon what Jesus has already done for us (John 3:16; Phil 3:9). Jesus died and rose again for the redemptive purpose of saving all people completely, in a way we could never save ourselves however hard we tried or however many good deeds we did. Our own human efforts to purify ourselves are so limited and erratic in comparison with the perfection of what Jesus has done for us (Col 1:13–14), as Oswald Chambers clearly explains:

> "I cannot save and sanctify myself; I cannot atone for sin; I cannot redeem the world; I cannot make right what is wrong, pure what is impure, holy what is unholy. That is all the sovereign work of God."[7]

7. Chambers, *My Utmost for His Highest*, October 9.

There is one greater than our own efforts or any law available to us. This is one of the key differences between Christianity and Buddhism.

That Jesus does all this for us is nothing but pure, unmerited grace: completely undeserved and freely given. "For it is by grace you have been saved, through faith—and this is not from yourselves, it is the gift of God" (Eph 2:8).

We have to come to the point where we realize that it is not about us and what we do but about Jesus and the redemptive work that he has already completed.

This was one of the things I found hardest to grasp when I became a Christian. Buddha taught his disciples to "be a refuge" to themselves but Jesus called me to abide deeply in him: "I am the vine; you are the branches. If you remain in me and I in you, you will bear much fruit; apart from me you can do nothing" (John 15:5).

At first, it felt too easy—a bit pathetic really—to just seek Jesus for it all when I was used to trying to do it for myself. But once I started to get a glimpse of what he had done for me, and to see that my efforts alone could never be enough, I gladly and willingly yielded to him.

As Buddhism does not acknowledge God, who can release forgiveness, those who believe in karma think that they have to live out the consequences of their past actions *themselves*, even through many lifetimes. However, Jesus died to obtain forgiveness for our sins even now: "If we confess our sins, he is faithful and just and will forgive us our sins and purify us from all unrighteousness" (1 John 1:9).

The blood of Jesus Christ that was shed on the cross has the power to wash and cleanse us instantly and completely. We are not bound to our past or present wrongdoings; we are set free from them. This is an incredible freedom available to us through Jesus.

The gospel of Jesus Christ offers help and hope in whatever situation we find ourselves in—even in the midst of suffering (Luke 4:18–19).

At times, I have the opportunity to visit some of the poorer churches in various parts of Thailand and speak to some of the Thai Christians there. Most of them were previously Buddhist. When I ask them about their lives, I've found they often respond in a similar way: "Were you born into a poor family?" "Yes, I'm poor." "Did you receive an education?" "No, I'm not well educated." "Do you think this is how it will be for you for the rest of your life?" "Oh yes, it will always be like this. It won't change."

Actually, these responses are Buddhist, not Christian!

I've found that an alarming number of Thai Christians have never clearly renounced Buddhism or Buddhist ways of thinking and still feel, even if only subconsciously, that they are working off the results of bad karma and so are destined to stay as they are because of it. At that point, I lead them in prayer to renounce Buddhism and Buddhist ways of thinking, which for most of them is deeply familiar and all they have known, so that the Lord can cleanse and free them of it. Jesus died not so that we should stay the same, or be trapped and defined by our social position or any lack in our past, but so that we should have fullness of life through him (John 10:10). It's often after such prayers that Thai Christians start to feel able to move forward from their past, no longer "fossilized" and held captive by it.

"Be transformed by the renewing of your mind. Then you will be able to test and approve what God's will is–his good, pleasing and perfect will" (Rom 12:2).

Prayer to empower a former Buddhist's will is usually necessary—and really helpful. This is especially so when passivity has set in through a long standing belief in karma and having emptiness and absence of desire as a spiritual goal. It certainly made a lot of difference to me. This prayer may well need to be repeated from time to time, until there is a clear rising up and out of lethargy and passivity. (Please see "Exploring Further 3: Prayer for the Empowering of Your Will" on page 122.)

Once I had become a Christian, my belief in karma evaporated immediately. To be honest, some aspects of it had always seemed a bit bizarre to me, even as a Buddhist, but as I had taken Buddhism so deeply on board and been so convinced by it, I had been willing to believe in karma, too. However, when God in his mercy opened my eyes to who Jesus is, that belief simply fell away.

For Thai Christians coming from Buddhist families, however, I've found that the pressure from relatives and peers to join in with certain Buddhist customs and traditions can present a big challenge. Often, these occasions involve making merit, and they are usually important social times, too. Great wisdom and discernment are needed in knowing which parts of Thai culture and tradition are okay for Thai Christians to participate in and which are not. (This is also true for Christians living in other nations/ cultures not having Christian foundations). It may well be that at such times they will need extra help and support—especially when they are new Christians.

In that regard, it is always easier in Thailand when a whole family comes to Christ (or at least the new Christian has a Christian friend), so that they can help each other to stand firm in the face of such pressure.

Ongoing solid Christian teaching and discipleship are essential for them to be able to mature and grow in their faith and to help them have a clear understanding of life from a biblical perspective. Strong bonds of Christian fellowship will also be a tremendous support for any former Buddhist.

I hope that reading about the Buddhist concept of karma and "making merit for the next life" will help in understanding why it so important to our Asian Buddhist friends, as well as giving you a greater understanding of Western Buddhists who may believe in karma and rebirth.

An important thing I have noticed—and it may be helpful for those sharing with Buddhists about Jesus to be aware of—is that most Buddhists would not be impressed with hearing about (the biblical understanding of) heaven. This is because Buddhists and Christians have very different concepts and understandings of what heaven(s) is/are.

God, being denied in Buddhism, has no place at all in Buddhist heavens. In Buddhism, these are considered to be the dwelling place of the gods, who, Buddha taught, are also subject to rebirth. Rebirth, even as a god, implies bondage in Buddhism, as Buddhists' ultimate goal is not to be reborn in any realm or state at all. So, the thought of "going to heaven" would have a negative connotation for them. It would be hard for them to grasp the idea of it as being good or an incentive. They would be trained and inclined to think that it's not enough, not as "high a goal" as being in a completely lifeless state of non-being.

The best way to share about Jesus with Buddhists, I have found, is under God's prompting and leading. When given the opportunity, I tend to focus on who Jesus is and the simple gospel message. Buddhists can't see Jesus. It's not that they are trying to be difficult—they simply can't see him. Pray that their spiritual eyes will be open to the one who has done it all for them already—that they can rest in the arms of their Creator and Redeemer, rather than struggle on isolated, by and in their own efforts.

Once a Buddhist has met with Jesus, they will begin to understand heaven correctly (Col 1:5); truly desirable rather than somewhere to avoid.

And if your Asian Buddhist friend does come to know Christ, unlike formerly as a Buddhist with their focus on doing "good actions" ("making merit"), *it is important that as a Christian they learn to receive from God first, in order to give, and not vice versa.*

For all former Buddhists, it is also extremely important that they renounce Buddhism and their Buddhist mindset clearly in prayer in Jesus' name, and that they also ask God to renew their minds. (For more details please see "Exploring Further 4: Prayer for Renouncing Buddhism, Idolatry, and/or the Occult" on page 123.)

Such prayers will help them be free to mature and develop in Christ. Otherwise, they may continue to be anchored down by a Buddhist mindset, as I have found with some Thai Christians coming out of Buddhism.

As we are beginning to realize, Buddhists and Christians see the world very differently. The next chapter will explore more of these differences.

Chapter 5

Impermanence, Suffering, No Self, or True Self

One of Buddha's central teachings that really grabbed me in my early Buddhist days is this: he considered everything—all phenomena, whether physical or mental—to have three characteristics. He said they were impermanent (*anicca*), unsatisfactory or prone to suffering (*dukkha*), and not belonging to a self or soul (*anatta*). For sure, these beliefs profoundly affected not only Buddha (whose primary quest in his spiritual life was to escape suffering) but also the millions who have followed him.

I'd like to share with you something of this teaching which, interestingly, I hardly ever remember being mentioned in popularized Buddhism and how I see it now as a Christian. As it is deep and complex, I won't be covering it extensively but will simply dip in and out of some relevant topics. Let's start with a quick look at "impermanence."

Buddha taught that all things are constantly changing—in a state of flux of momentary arising and disappearing. This is how it was expressed in words attributed to him when talking to a teacher named Araka:

> "O Brāhmaṇa, it is just like a mountain river, flowing far and swift, taking everything along with it; there is no moment, no instant, no second when it stops flowing, but it goes on flowing and continuing. So Brāhmaṇa, is human life, like a mountain river."[1]

1. Rahula, op. cit., 25–26.

Regarding nirvāṇa, although ever elusive and notoriously difficult to define, the Pali Canon uses such adjectives as "everlasting" (*accanta*) and "endless" (*ananta*) which imply that it is considered to be permanent.

We find acknowledgement of change in the Bible, too, although it is not treated as an important doctrine, as in Buddhism, and does not arrive at the same conclusions. Perhaps most famous is the passage in Ecclesiastes 3, a small part of which is quoted below from verses 1–3 (nkjv):

> "To everything there is a season,
> A time for every purpose under heaven:
>> A time to be born,
>> And a time to die;
>> A time to plant,
>> And a time to pluck what is planted;
>> A time to kill,
>> And a time to heal;
>> A time to break down,
>> And a time to build up."

There is also frequent reference in Scripture to that which is permanent/everlasting: for example, God himself (Gen 21:33), God's Word (Isa 40:8), and everlasting life with him (John 3:16).

Not only did Buddha conclude that all things are impermanent but that ""Whatever is impermanent is *dukkha*" (*Yad aniccaṃ taṃ dukkhaṃ*)."[2] —*dukkha* means unsatisfactory or prone to suffering.

While acknowledging that there is suffering, Christianity does not teach that everything is prone to it, nor does it emphasize the need to escape suffering in the same way Buddhism does. The Christian approach and response to suffering are very different. As the following story shows, Jesus can meet us even in extreme suffering and use it for his own redemptive purposes.

"For the Lord is a God of justice." (Isa 30:18)

One of the saddest and most challenging times I've ever had to face in Thailand occurred when I'd been living there for about three years, when I

---

2. Rahula, op. cit., 25.

was unusually busy. We were in the early stages of establishing the discipleship ministry, I had just moved house and was about to go to Australia for a ten-day mission trip. I felt stretched. I'd barely taken things out of their boxes in my new home in Bangkok, and now I had to pack to go away.

It was then that I received some urgent phone calls from a Thai Christian who I didn't know. She was asking if I could go and pray for a Thai teenager called Anchalee who had been sexually abused. Regrettably, my sense of my "professional boundaries" took over and I replied: "Can she wait until I get back from my trip? I will come and see her then as soon as I can." Being Thai and socially very gracious, this woman agreed.

On my return, I promptly got in touch with her and was shocked to hear that in the last few days Anchalee had made a serious attempt at suicide by jumping off a high place and was critically ill in hospital with brain damage. She had an operation but was now in intensive care and her prospects were really not good.

On hearing more of Anchalee's story, I discovered that it was unbelievably sad. She was a Christian from the provinces (the countryside outside of the big cities) who had been repeatedly raped as a child by her father for many years and had been made pregnant by him. Her parents were not Christian but she had heard about Jesus through a Thai Christian radio program, which had sown hope in her heart that Jesus could help her.

She contacted the local church and explained her situation to the pastor there, and from time to time she would flee to the church for refuge. But, horrendous as her situation was, the church's leaders failed to help her to find a way out.

Desperate for help, she went to the police. I was given a copy of the police report. It was extremely hard to read. In fact, I could only manage to read a little at a time as the contents were so dark. I had no reason to believe that Anchalee was making these things up, and she had no history of mental illness that I knew of. It was so sad to realize what a catalog of horrors she had lived though.

While I had been away, she had been put into a government home; but she was taunted by the other young people, she very much wanted to leave, and became suicidal.

Though there are some wonderful mothers in Thailand, unbelievably, Anchalee's own mother did not support her. She was in denial, angry, and blamed her daughter. I heard that she accused Anchalee of trying to break up the family, of bringing disgrace on them, and causing them to lose face in their village. Not for a moment, it seems, did she try to understand her daughter's terrible situation.

It seemed to me that Anchalee had no justice from anywhere. So many people—including, I realized, me—had let her down. There was no one that I could see who had been there to protect or support her.

I went to visit her in intensive care with the woman who had rung me originally and another Thai Christian woman. Anchalee lay still with her eyes closed as we gathered around her in silence, aware of the gravity of her condition.

After a little while, we started to quietly sing worship songs. Then, one of the Thai women prayed for Anchalee, assuring her of God's love for her. The Lord's presence was with us and, sad and grief-stricken as we were for her, it felt such a privilege to be with this very vulnerable one, toward the end of her young life.

Drawing close to Anchalee, I bent down, and prayed in Jesus name. I told her how sorry we were that in this world she had had no justice. I assured her, though, that Jesus was her justice and defense and that she would find her justice in him, even now as she looked to him.

Until that point she had not seemed to respond, but now her tears slowly fell, running down her checks. Bruised and battered as she was, mentally, physically, and emotionally, she had met with Jesus and her spirit could recognize it.

"For the Lord is righteous, he loves justice; the upright will see his face." (Ps 11:7)

Some days later, we heard that Anchalee had died. But *we had witnessed that right in the face of the devastating consequences of sin, Jesus, through the power of his risen life, had come, himself embodying and administering the justice, mercy, peace, and love that no one and nothing else could bring.*

How could this be? Having risen from the dead, Jesus is alive and ever present to enter into our lives. He said: "I am the Living One; I was dead, and now look, I am alive for ever and ever! And I hold the keys of death and Hades" (Rev 1:18).

What an incredible source of help in time of need.

Buddha, though, is dead, he did not rise again; his goal was to be extinguished forever. This has great significance spiritually. And I think it helps to explain the world's high number of folk Buddhists who seek help elsewhere, such as from spirits, idols, and the occult in times of trouble and need. However much respect they have for Buddha, they know that when the pressure is on he is nowhere to be found.

Some years ago in Hong Kong, I heard of one of our team who was concerned about a street sleeper who had a very bad cough.

"Can I pray for you?" she said to him. He replied: "I'm a Buddhist!" She said, "I'd like to pray for you, that Jesus will heal your cough." "But I'm a Buddhist," he repeated. "Well," she said, "Buddha is dead, but Jesus is alive. Can I pray for you?" And finally he said, "Yes."

God in his mercy healed this man's cough, and then he came to believe in Jesus, seeing that Jesus is alive but Buddha is dead.

Here, Martin Kamphuis shares his experience on the some of the differences in approach to suffering of Buddha and Jesus:

"*If I compare a statue of Buddha sunk in silent meditation with the shattering image of pain seen in the suffering man Christ Jesus on the cross—what a contrast! Initially after trusting Christ I didn't want to take this image on board. It was so contrary to all that I had learned and considered worth striving for. . . .*

"*Jesus Christ . . . does not reveal himself to me in a glorious enlightened figure like Buddha, but in this pathetic, suffering condition.* But I had to admit, this image of suffering somehow appealed to me more. It corresponded to my condition and the condition of the world. Even *Buddha taught 'To live is to suffer.' But he had fled from the world's suffering. He had distanced himself far from man's suffering. Clearly Jesus hadn't done that. . . .*

"Up till then, I could not and would not believe or admit that in Jesus Christ God had carried such a burden for me, thereby showing me his love and his desire for fellowship with me. . . . My misery and his love met at the cross.

"*With God it's not a case of 'to live is to suffer,' but 'God himself bears my suffering and gives me life.' Through a screaming image of suffering God has built a bridge towards me.* I understood it—the chasm has been bridged! Tears rolled down my cheeks. At last I had found a place where my failures, my rebellion and my guilt could be laid aside."[3]

3. Kamphuis, *Ich war Buddhist*, 194–197, emphasis mine.

Finally, to complete this central teaching of the Buddha, he concluded not only that all things are impermanent and so are prone to suffering but also that we have no self or soul (*anicca, dukkha, anatta*).

What did he mean by that?

In his analysis of human beings, he found nothing in us that he recognized as a self or soul (*anatta*). In fact, he outright denied that we have either, saying they were imaginary and false. Buddha considered us to be no more than a combination of ever-changing and unsatisfactory mental and physical "phenomena," which he divided into five groups ("aggregates"): matter, sensations, perceptions, mental formations, and consciousness.

And although he recognized consciousness as an aspect of our humanity, Buddha taught that it should not be taken as "spirit," in opposition to matter,[4] making it clear that he did not believe we have a spirit either.

To quote Rahula again: "What we call a 'being,' or an 'individual,' or 'I,' is only a convenient name or a label given to the combination of these five groups."[5] "There is nothing behind them that can be called a permanent Self (*Ātman*), individuality, or anything that can in reality be called 'I.'"[6]

As Buddhaghosa, a famous Sinhalese Buddhist monk who wrote commentaries on the *Tipiṭaka*—Theravāda Buddhist doctrine, said:

> "Mere suffering exists, but no sufferer is found;
> The deeds are, but no doer is found."[7]

While I was living in the Buddhist temple, we often used to talk impersonally when referring to ourselves, in order to support this idea of "no self." For instance: "I have a pain in *the* knee" and "I will go to *the* room," rather than "I have a pain in *my* knee" and "I will go to *my* room." Developing such a view plays a key role in Buddhist thought and outlook, powerfully changing the way we see both ourselves and the world.

Even as a Buddhist, though, I began to have my doubts. I felt that there were unexplained paradoxes in this teaching. Although Buddha clearly denied that we have a self, he taught that liberation comes from our own

4. Rahula, op. cit., 23.
5. Rahula, op. cit., 25.
6. Ibid., 26.
7. Ibid., 26.

efforts alone. He also said that ultimately there is no one who suffers to whom he tries to offer a remedy!

So, when I became a Christian, how did I come to understand that I have a self, a soul, and a spirit?

Once I was no longer alienated from God having met with Jesus, the realization that I had a self, a soul, and a spirit naturally came along with it too. My belief in Buddha's doctrine of "no self" simply vanished, unable to hold me any more.

Actually, in retrospect, I felt like it was harder work trying to deny that I had a self than embracing it! It did take me a while, though, to start feeling comfortable with talking about "myself" and "my" things. So engrained had the Buddhist way of thinking and speaking become that at times I needed to consciously train myself out of it.

So, let's look at the Christian viewpoint.

Here, the Christian author A. W. Tozer writes beautifully on the "self-hood" of God:

"A more positive assertion of selfhood could not be imagined than those words of God to Moses: I AM THAT I AM [Exod 3:14]. Everything God is . . . is set forth in that unqualified declaration of independent being. Yet in God, self is not sin but the quintessence of all possible goodness, holiness and truth."[8]

Jesus, too, declares his "selfhood" (and shows that he has been ever-present) when he says: "before Abraham was, I am" (John 8:58 nkjv).

Jesus also clearly speaks of having a soul and spirit. As he predicts his death on the cross, he says: "Now my soul is troubled" (John 12:27). And just before he dies he says: "Father, into your hands I commit my spirit" (Luke 23:46).

God the Father, when blessing the people of Israel, speaks of having a heart and soul when he says: "I will rejoice over them to do them good, and I will assuredly plant them in this land, with all My heart[9] and with all My soul" (Jer 32:41 nkjv).

8. Tozer, *The Knowledge of the Holy*, 29.

9. It may be worth mentioning that in Buddhism the word for "heart," *citta*, is also used for "mind," with an emphasis on the emotive side of the mind. Whereas, according to the NIV Study Bible commentary on Psalm 4:7: "In biblical language [the heart denotes] the center of the human spirit, from which spring emotions, thought, motivations, courage and action—'the wellspring of life' (Pr 4:23)" (*The NIV Study Bible*, 773).

Scripture tells us that we are made in the image of God (Gen 1:26) and makes it clear that God has given us a self, soul, and spirit. In 1 Thessalonians 5:23, we read of the Apostle Paul blessing some believers before his departure: "May your whole spirit, soul and body be kept blameless at the coming of our Lord Jesus Christ."

Whereas Buddha taught that the self is illusory, a result of "ignorance," through Jesus we find *our true self*. This, in Scripture means our "new" self (Eph 4:24), "new creation" (2 Cor 5:17), as opposed to the broken, sinful self (Rom 6:3–16; Eph 4:22–23). Once we have been brought alive through a relationship with Jesus where he is centered in us (John 17:23) and we are in him (John 15:4), we find our true home. Here, there is room for our real, integrated, and emancipated self or "I" to fully develop; one that is capable, in a godly way, of imagining and feeling, of hearing and responding to God, the source of true meaning and creativity.

I cannot imagine a better way to explain our true self than how Oswald Chambers does:

> "God is the only One who has the right to myself and when I love Him with all my heart and soul and mind and strength, self in its essence is realized."[10]

I have seen it in myself, and I see it in other Buddhists who come to know Jesus: suddenly, "more of them" appears, as their personality, character, likes, and dislikes that God gave them now have permission to express themselves and develop.

After I had disrobed and was no longer living under the monastic rules, I was free to do those things I'd always loved: drive a car, ride a horse, and occasionally to relish in a high tea in the afternoon! I was enjoying freedom in Jesus—not freedom to sin but freedom to embrace life. As we are called into life by our Creator and find our true home within, we are able truly to celebrate life; it's like black-and-white TV suddenly turning into color!

I would go so far as to say that when our hearts are not responsive to this greater life in God, it is as if we cease to be. I imagine it was something like this that happened to Buddha. His self, his soul, and his spirit could easily be denied when he had no knowledge of or relationship with God to call and "ignite" them into being.

10. Chambers, *Still Higher for His Highest*, July 16.

There are consequences to such beliefs, though, and I feel a better explanation of the extreme danger of denying that we have a soul would be hard to find than this:

> "In failing to recognize the full soul that is another person, we in effect X out all that is uniquely human about that person's creation. We delete the human. . . . persons are robbed of the great privilege of coming present to their own hearts and there—in the presence of God—finally coming to understand who they are. . . . and just as tragically, all that is positive within that soul and unique to its creation as a human being will be overlooked. Through ignoring the good, it will go unaffirmed, and, in effect, denied existence. It will not be called into life."[11]

I'm curious, and have found myself trying to imagine, how Buddha could have arrived at the conclusion that we have no self, no soul, no spirit. What would it take to get there? Please excuse my indulgence as I briefly share what I feel may have contributed to this.

Christians speak of thinking and being, reason and faith, "head knowledge" and "heart knowledge," making a distinction between the understanding that comes from the conscious, scientific, reasoning mind ("the head") on the one hand and the imaginative, feeling way of knowing ("the heart")—such as faith—on the other.

These two ways of knowing are very different, but both carry great importance. However, a dreadful rift and imbalance can arise between our head and heart which powerfully distort our understanding. Leanne Payne talks of this as "the schism we moderns suffer due to the false separation between reason and faith, that which is behind the elevation of the rational faculty (making it to be the whole mind) and the denigration and even denial of the intuitive, feeling mind."[12]

As we have seen, Buddha functioned predominantly from his rational, analytical, scientific mind, but was this (as Leanne Payne puts it) to "the denigration and even denial" of his "intuitive feeling mind"?

Uninformed by the wisdom of the heart, some key aspects of our humanity (our self, soul, and spirit) can easily be "analyzed away" and so discounted. To such scientific mindsets, of people both ancient and modern—and once including me!—Buddhism may well appeal.

11. Payne, *Restoring the Christian Soul*, 207.
12. Payne, *The Healing Presence*, 158.

Please do not misunderstand me, our intellects, our rational, and scientific minds can be a great blessing. What is needed, though, is a true integration, a balance of head and heart, thinking and being, reason and faith. When that comes together under God, we see something truly beautiful, which points us to the substantial and real.

How does this help you in understanding and reaching your Buddhist friend?

From my experience of ministry in Thailand, I have found that many Buddhists come from a family in which there has been a strong influence of Buddhism for generations. It is no small thing for someone to be taught from early on that they have no self, that everything is impermanent and unsatisfactory, and that their highest spiritual goal is not to be or exist in any form. *It has powerful consequences upon them and their humanity.*

I was talking about this recently to Malee, a Thai Bible student in England. She commented (and I have noticed, as well) that it's not uncommon for Thai people to feel empty, lonely, and unaffirmed, which leaves them really hungry for security and connection. She went on to say that the desperation that follows easily leads to fallen attempts to try to "fill" and comfort themselves. These feelings, I would say, are definitely exacerbated by Buddhist teachings.

One of my close Thai Christian friends told me she was not able to let go of her addictions until she met with the love of Father God. She is someone who has really blossomed and matured in her Christian faith, and as a person, as she has spent time with God.

In helping former Buddhists who become Christians, from the East or the West, I have found they benefit greatly from prayer to come into a closer relationship with Father God. Whether they are being prayed for by others or are praying alone, learning to simply abide in Jesus, receive his love, and be filled by him (Eph 3:19), will give them great inner strength.

We can pray, too, that God will name them, show them who they really are, and affirm them as his sons and daughters. Such prayers are like water in the desert, their true selves, characters, and personalities, as God made them, are called into life, blessed, and affirmed as they spend time in his presence.

Christianity is about embracing life fully, in a godly way, rather than persistently trying to let it go and detach from it. Enjoying wholesome activities together with others, such as going for walks or eating together, in themselves nurture us and give us a sense of belonging.

Developing godly relationships and friendships where Jesus is clearly central is another important part of maturing in faith.

Learning to serve others will also bring us a sense of wellbeing. Mother Theresa of Calcutta said that this was a great cure for depression, as it involves focusing outside of ourselves to the needs of others, rather than focusing on ourselves.

Having taken a quick look at these important Buddhist teachings, in the next chapter I will explore a bit further the nature of Buddhism.

Chapter 6

The Illusory and Insubstantial Nature of Evil

"Such is the destiny of all who forget God; so perishes the hope of the godless. What they trust in is fragile; what they rely on is a spider's web. They lean on the web, but it gives way; they cling to it, but it does not hold." (Job 8:13–15)

"There are two major problems: first, to recognize evil as evil, and to combat it; but even more difficult, the problem of recognizing evil where it simulates what is good (1 John 4:1; 2 Cor 11:14, 15).
. . .
   "The strategy of the Devil is always the same: to empty incarnational reality [Christ's transforming presence] of its inner weight; then to simulate the goodness associated with incarnational reality, even though the reality is not there. Once a person chooses that simulation, even perhaps basing his life on it, he has been hooked by emptiness that has been given the look of fullness. A person has based his life on something that never existed."[1]

Something happened during those last months in the Buddhist temple that has really fascinated me and which I feel holds great significance. Let me explain.

---

1. John R. Sheets in his foreword to Leanne Payne's, *Real Presence*, 14.

I was powerfully touched through seeing a video in the temple of Jackie Pullinger and her helpers in Hong Kong who were praying for drug addicts and the poor in the name of Jesus and by the power of the Holy Spirit and seeing them healed. And, even though I was still a Buddhist nun, I started to battle at times with intense confusion, not really sure any more if I was a Christian or a Buddhist. Gradually, over some very uncomfortable months, I witnessed the disappearance of my strong Buddhist faith. Now I knew that Jesus was real and I wanted to be free to worship God.

As I explained in *I Once Was a Buddhist Nun*: "For thirteen years Buddha's teaching had felt like a mountain of truth standing solidly behind me. When I came to know Christ, that mountain collapsed into a pile of dust and rubbish."[2]

Not long after I had left the temple, I realized that I did not actually know any other Theravāda Buddhist monks or nuns who had become Christians. In that respect I felt quite alone in my experience—that was until, a few years later, when I met Paul (whose story I tell in *I Once Was a Buddhist Nun*).

Paul had called me a couple of times from the temple while he was still a Buddhist monk but after God had touched him. I found talking to him really reassuring, as much of what he was going through was very similar to my own experience when I had seriously begun to doubt Buddhism. To quote from his story:

> "He too had been extremely confused, at times really not knowing what was happening to him. He was surprised—as I had been— that the Buddha's teaching, which for so long had appeared so real and meaningful to him, like a 'solid mountain,' had suddenly collapsed into a pile of rubbish compared to knowing Christ. He asked me where it had gone to."[3]

(What had happened to us put me in mind of what the Apostle Paul says in Phil 3:7–9.)

As we chatted, I was able to share with him those things that had helped me when I was in the same position:

- to focus on Jesus as much as he could, as I knew this would restore his peace and his balance whenever he lost them;

2. Baker, *I Once Was a Buddhist Nun*, 88.
3. Ibid., 118–119.

- to worship God, in songs of praise or words of worship;

- to pray and read the Bible.

I told him that some friends and I would be praying for him, too.

What I found so interesting as we shared together was that I could see a pattern emerging. Both of us had at times experienced great confusion. Plus, we'd witnessed the collapse of a faith in Buddhism that had been so strong we had been willing to give our lives to it. Now it simply couldn't be found any more.

Where had it gone to? What was going on?

Understanding this, I feel, is crucial to understanding the true nature of Buddhism. In answer I would say that its illusory and insubstantial nature had been exposed. Now we could see it for what it really is.

As I looked for keys to unlock this further, these two areas began to stand out for me as being really relevant:

- a clear biblical understanding of the true nature of evil

- an understanding of the nature of reality

First, then, what does the Bible say about the characteristics of evil? Here are some pointers, with some extremely helpful insights from Leanne Payne:

1. It counterfeits truth, as there is no truth in it.

   "According to the Scriptures, Satan is the master counterfeiter, the "god" of this world, and the one through whom the diabolical revelations come that plague the mind of man and show up in his myths, his philosophies, his theologies, and his psychologies."[4]

   "Satan . . . deceives the whole world" (Rev 12:9b nkjv).

2. It is illusory.

   "Evil has an illusory nature. It attempts to win through bluff—through puffing itself up to horrendous size. But one word of truth, spoken in the power of the Holy Spirit, solid as a rock and splendid as eternity, flies swift as the surest arrow to puncture evil's swelled balloon of lies, posturing, and bravado."[5]

   That "which is not" can have people in bondage: "The beast [an instrument of Satan] who once was, and now is not" (Rev 17:11a).

4. Payne, *Real Presence*, 157.
5. Payne, *Listening Prayer*, 115.

3. It is insubstantial.

"Because the malevolence of Satan and the fallen angels cannot create but only destroy, they continually fall toward the nothingness they have chosen, toward what is ultimately insubstantial."[6]

Please see Job 8:13–15 at the beginning of this chapter.

4. It hates reality and is not in accordance with it, and distracts us from that which is real.

Evil provides an alternative and ultimately false world: "*In one sense, evil is finally the highest unreality.*"[7]

"The working of Satan, with all power, signs and lying wonders and with all unrighteous deception" (2 Thess 2:9b–10a NKJV).

5. It hates all that is created and seeks to confuse, defile, and destroy.

"Satan and his minions hate all that is created: all of Nature, the very *matter* that goes to make up our world, our minds and bodies. The Satanic aim is to twist, defile, and destroy us—spirit, soul, and body."[8]

"The thief comes only to steal and kill and destroy" (John 10:10a).

Evil ultimately dehumanizes people. It seeks to destroy us—even Jesus (see Matt 4:5–6).

6. It leads to nothingness, emptiness.

"When Satan turned to evil, he turned to "what was not," to non-being, to nothingness, to nonsense. His bent will could only oppose God by destroying, by striving after nothingness. Likewise, when man chooses evil, he is finally choosing nothingness—that which will only hurt himself and those around him."[9]

"They went far from Me and walked after emptiness and became empty" (Jer 2:5b NASB).

7. It rejects God's will and way, separating us from him, our true selves, and others.

6. Payne, *Real Presence*, 30.
7. Ibid., 152, emphasis mine.
8. Payne, *The Healing Presence*, 85.
9. Payne, *Real Presence*, 151.

"Evil, theologically speaking, is separation from God—and in that condition, separation from our fellows, the good earth, and all creation as well. Evil, psychologically speaking, is separation within ourselves. In truth, the fallen self cannot know itself."[10]

"They did not receive the love of the truth, that they might be saved. And for this reason God will send them strong delusion, that they should believe the lie, that they all may be condemned who did not believe the truth" (2 Thess 2:10b–12a NKJV).

As I became more aware of the characteristics of evil, I realized to my amazement that they were clearly describing my experience and giving me an answer to it. I have not found any other explanation elsewhere.

Not all Buddhists are like I was in this regard, but my heart was very strongly against God, both before I became a Buddhist and for the most part while I was one. I could recognize that. I remember when in a pub one night with some friends in my pre-Buddhist days, claiming to be a "daughter of Satan," which of course I have clearly renounced since becoming a Christian. Had I unwittingly, with Buddhism, continued to give myself over to spiritual darkness?

When I saw Buddhism dissolve in the light of Christ, I had to acknowledge that I *had* been living under spiritual deception for all of those years—bound and committed to a lie, a mere appearance of truth that in reality did not exist at all (Isa 28:15b).

So, how did evil come to exist? The Bible shows us that evil coming into our world was a consequence of the fall. It speaks of it as being initiated and willed by Satan who is known by many names, including "the devil" (1 John 3:8), "the evil one" (John 17:15), "the tempter" (Matt 4:3) and "the great dragon" (Rev 12:9). (For more names of both Jesus and his enemy, please see "Exploring Further 5" on page 125).

Satan is depicted as always hostile to God, seeking to overthrow both his purposes and his people (1 Pet 5:8). He is a liar, "not holding to the truth, for there is no truth in him. When he lies, he speaks his native language, for he is a liar and the father of lies" (John 8:44). Though in reality he is the prince of darkness, he masquerades as an angel of light (2 Cor 11:14). Those who choose to follow Satan rather than God, come under the dominion of that which is false, illusory, and dark.

10. Payne, *The Healing Presence*, 58.

Scripture describes Satan's end as the final Day of the Lord approaches:

> "The lawless one will be revealed, whom the Lord will consume with the breath of His mouth and destroy with the brightness of His coming." (2 Thess 2:8 nkjv)

Second, there is the nature of reality.

For sure, just as John Sheets described in the quote at the beginning of this chapter, I had been "hooked by emptiness that [had] been given the look of fullness" and had "based [my] life on something that never existed."

It became evident to me that what the teachings and practices of Buddhism had led me to believe was reality had proved in the end, in the light of Christ, to have no substance. I had been completely deceived—Buddhism, a master of disguises, so adept at hiding its real nature.

In comparison, over the last twenty-two years the Christian experience and understanding of reality have proved to me to be completely substantial and real. I've been able to fully stand on it, depend on it, knowing it won't give way. Surely I can rejoice, along with the psalmist David, that God "set my feet on a rock and gave me a firm place to stand" (Ps 40:2b).

Or as Oswald Chambers puts it: "Nothing can ever upset God or the almighty Reality of Redemption."[11]

Having watched Buddhism collapse around me, I would now say without any doubt that the Buddhist and Christian experience and teaching of reality are truly poles apart.

So, if we are not to get caught out, how do we discern the real from the unreal, truth from a lie? I have learned that we need to see: is it able to stand in God's light and presence, or does it disappear as above?

Looking back, how do I understand the process of the "unraveling" of my Buddhist faith? The following describes, at least in part, what I believe happened during those last months in the temple (which I feel is reflected in Paul's story, too):

As truth—God's presence in me by his Holy Spirit—entered, I began to extricate myself from the evil web of lies that had kept me from reality, and so the battle began. The great mental confusion which at times sent me "spinning," and made it so hard for me to see what was really going on,

---

11. Chambers, *My Utmost for His Highest*, December 3.

came to the surface from time to time, giving me glimpses of the intensity of the battle within and the power by which I was held.

For freedom, I needed to choose reality over the illusion, the truth over the lie, life over death, heaven over hell. I so needed God's help, and much courage, to give up the old and familiar, however much it continued to pull at me and sow doubts that I was wrong, in order to be able to walk away from it. The enemy's desire, I have since learnt, is always to overpower people's minds, because then it is easy to control the whole person.

Truly it was an act of faith, fuelled by God's grace, to keep choosing Jesus in the heat of it. As I did so, I witnessed what had once seemed so solid and real disintegrate before my eyes. This great illusion of truth that had opposed God with its goal of nothingness and no more becoming, now shattered:

> "For this purpose the Son of God was manifested, that He might destroy the works of the devil." (1 John 3:8b nkjv)

Little did I realize that there were Christians praying for me at this crucial time, or how empowered I was being by their prayers! Only later did I discover who they were, and to this day I am so grateful to them.

> "Hate what is evil; cling to what is good." (Rom 12:9b)

Having experienced the illusory and insubstantial nature of Buddhism, the Lord Jesus brought me to the great reality and substantiality of what is real and good.

Just as Jesus said to the Apostle Paul at his conversion,

> "I now send you . . . to open their eyes, in order to turn them from darkness to light, and from the power of Satan to God, that they may receive forgiveness of sins and an inheritance among those who are sanctified by faith in Me." (Acts 26:17b–18 nkjv)

So, too, Jesus had opened my eyes, and turned me from darkness to light, from the power of Satan to God.

In coming to God, I was really blessed by these words of Jesus that speak of being reconciled to the Father: "I am in my Father, and you are in me, and I am in you" (John 14:20). Christ is with me and in me, my power to be and my hope of glory (Col 1:27), my way of knowing and being linked to ultimate truth and reality.

God's revelation of himself to us is to experience the real: that which cannot and will not fade away or disintegrate (Heb 7:16). And by living according to God's Word we remain living in reality (John 14:21).

Leanne Payne describes it this way:

> "The Christian view is one of man the creature fully reconciled to God the Creator. To be thus reconciled (healed, restored, forgiven, and loved) is to know the Good."[12]

In living out my Christian faith, I have found that the experience of coming to know God, deeply personal as it may be, is not a matter of staying closeted away alone with him—though there can be a time for that. Even during my last few months as a Buddhist nun, I longed to be in church with others, to pray and be baptized, even though I didn't really understand why or what it meant! It's not only our relationship with God that he wants to restore and bless, but our relationship with other people, too, whether believers (Heb 10:25) or those outside the church (Mark 12:31; Rom 12:18).

So, how did my understanding of evil as a Christian differ from what I had previously been taught as a Buddhist?

In a nutshell: I would say they are very different, and so, they are really not comparable.

Buddha did speak of evil; of "Māra, the evil one," who is often portrayed in Buddhist texts and art like a "demon" trying to tempt Buddha away from his spiritual path. Although its meaning goes wider than this, it is certainly not the same as the Christian teaching and understanding of Satan, even if both are described as "the evil one."

As the Buddhist monk and scholar Walpola Sri Rahula wrote:

> "The root of all evil is ignorance (*avijjā*) and false views (*micchā diṭṭhi*)."[13]

So, according to Buddha, "ignorance" (of the way things really are) and "false views" are the root of all evil and what is needed to be overcome, which is obviously different from the Christian understanding.

I hope and pray that these stories and reflections will assist in enabling you to see more clearly the true nature of Buddhism, the reality of

---

12. Payne, *Real Presence*, 46–47.
13. Rahula, *What the Buddha Taught*, 3.

its bondage, and the tremendous struggle there can be to come out of it. Beyond its harmless looking appearance, there is actually a very real battle for souls going on.

If we don't understand its true nature, Buddhism may easily fascinate and intrigue even some Christians. To those Christians who are drawn to it, tempted to embrace aspects of Buddhist meditation or teaching in their own lives, whether directly from Buddhism or mixed with Christian practices, I would like to bring a real caution. Buddhism is not at all compatible with Christianity, nor can it add to it in any way. Inclusion of any aspect of it will, in the end, serve only to weaken and confuse you in your Christian faith (see 1 Tim 4:1).

As the prayer in the Anglican Church says: "The Lord bless us, and preserve us from all evil, and keep us in eternal life. Amen."

So, how does this help you to understand and reach your Buddhist friend?

As we have seen, praying for them is essential. It may be that you will be called on to pray for them day or night, as God leads. It is important to know that your prayers may be as crucial to their freedom just as my friends' prayers were for me.

In looking at its illusory and insubstantial nature, I have taken what I would imagine to be a little-explored view of Buddhism. We won't stop there, though. Let's venture further and ask: Is Buddhism a form of idolatry?

Chapter 7

One God or Many gods?

"Our Lord is above all gods." (Ps 135:5b nkjv)

It was a hot and sticky afternoon in central Bangkok. I hadn't been living there long and was on my way to the British embassy to meet some friends who worked there. Arriving early, I was able to take a few moments to relax wandering around the embassy grounds. It felt so good to enjoy some lush greenery in this somewhat polluted, traffic-filled city.

Then, to my surprise, in the middle of the grounds, I came across a large, impressive statue of Queen Victoria. To be honest, it felt good to see a statue of one of "my" queens, especially in Thailand. There are so many statues and pictures of the much revered Thai king and queen (and former Thai monarchs) all over the country that, with all due respect, it felt like a pleasant change.

I was enjoying looking at her, sitting there rather grandly with her famously dour expression, when all of a sudden my heart sank: "Oh, no! How can it be? Not here, please! Not to Queen Victoria!"

My eye had fallen on some offerings of flowers at her feet and a garland round her neck that, I imagine, a Thai person—probably a folk Buddhist—had placed there; such offerings as would be given to an idol.

My carefree enjoyment disappeared in an instant. This was Queen Victoria, not an idol! She was a Christian and, even though a queen, she knew and confessed that she was in submission to a greater King—her God and Maker—the "KING OF KINGS AND LORD OF LORDS" (Rev 19:16), Jesus Christ, to whom she willingly bowed her knee.

These offerings at her feet and round her neck were going far beyond mere respect. This was not the same, for instance, as a little child giving the queen a posy of flowers in admiration and love for her; this was idolatrous worship of the queen herself, as if she were a goddess, able to bestow blessings and good fortune on the one giving the offerings!

Hmm, I wonder if Queen Victoria would be amused to be venerated in this way, I thought to myself.

"Definitely not," I quickly concluded. This certainly is not a matter for amusement. On the contrary, it points to something really very significant. This misbegotten attempt to deify Queen Victoria raised a question that we all need to settle: Where does our worship and source of hope lie: in something or someone created or in the Creator himself?

> "As G. K. Chesterton once pointed out: when [people] cease to believe in God they do not then believe in nothing. They then become capable of believing anything."[1]

Great, though, the difference between whom the queen and her "devotee" were giving their veneration, what they had in common is that they both desired to worship. It seems to me that this deep desire and need to worship is inherent within our humanity and comes from deep within, whether we are aware of it or not. It's not so much a matter of whether or not we worship but rather who or what it is that we worship. One thing is for sure: our hearts are hungry, and their needs will be met. Where God is not known, we will find something or someone to worship.

So, who is this God that Queen Victoria worshiped? He is the Creator of all things (see Gen 1:1–2:4); he is not a part of creation. He spoke them all into being, and holds them all together.

Although creation had a beginning, God has always been (Ps 90:2; Isa 40:28), he is now and he will always be (Rev 1:4).

He is the only true God. He said: "Before Me there was no God formed, nor shall there be after Me" (Isa 43:10b nkjv). He was before all other gods and, unlike them, God is love and is loveable, he knows us and is knowable. He is not a lifeless statue to worship or a philosophy to study, he is a living

---

1. O'Brien, "Harry Potter and the Paganization of Children's Culture," 12.

God who loves us deeply and wants us for himself, undividedly. In no way is he willing to share us with idols!

This deep desire we have to worship, I would say, is given to us by God, for himself (Eccl 3:11b). And in knowing God personally we are freed to live in the safety and wisdom of his ways.

Even Queen Victoria in her pre-eminent and powerful position could humble herself before God—One she knew to be far greater and to whom she knew she was answerable. Her many letters and journals are punctuated by prayers and deference that give honor to God. I can't in any way imagine that she would have desired to solicit idolatrous worship from anyone *for herself!*

"Keep yourself from idols." (1 John 5:21)

You may ask, then, why anyone would want to worship a queen. Strange as it may seem to some, it happens to be normal practice for many Thais who believe that their kings can be more than mere humans and may be worshiped as "gods" (an ideal borrowed from Hinduism). Worshiping them (for instance, the much loved former kings who have done many helpful things for the country) involves paying respects, giving offerings, and seeking blessings, help, or good luck in times of need.

This tendency to make "gods" of kings (or other impressive people) is really nothing new. Since ancient times it has raised its head, most often in cultures where God is not known. We find examples of it in the Bible. In Old Testament times, in Canaanite culture, the heads of clans, tribes, or cities were highly venerated by following generations and often received the title of "gods" (Ps 82:1–8). And in New Testament times, people were expected not only to be loyal to Rome politically but also to worship Caesar as a god.

From early historical records it appears that the Thais have long been involved in some kind of idolatry. They were originally animists, believing that good and bad spirits existed all around them, i.e., in every house, tree, and hill. They appeased and sought protection from these spirits with offerings such as flowers, candles, incense, and food.

They later adopted Buddhism and nowadays most Thais would identify themselves primarily as Buddhist; but the vast majority are folk Buddhists and only a few practice strictly the more traditional form of Buddhism, such as the one I was involved in. Even today, many Thais are still taught to fear and respect spirits by their parents and other relatives from early on in their lives. "Spirit houses" can be seen outside (and sometimes inside) most houses and buildings in Thailand, where, at many of them, regular offerings are made—a practice that does not come from Buddhism. It is also common for Thais to have a deep rooted fear of ghosts.

It is not only spirits they seek to please—as anyone who lives in Thailand will tell you—most Thai people embrace an unbelievable *mixture* of spiritual practices as well as Buddhism, including the worship of idols of various kinds, widespread use of the occult, and Brahmanism. This gives a clear illustration of the power to assimilate and absorb other local beliefs and indigenous religions that folk Buddhism possesses, that I mentioned in chapter 1.

One of my Thai friends told me that many folk Buddhists in Thailand don't seem to be fussy about what the idol or statue actually is. If they regard it as a "sacred object," or it means something to them personally, that is enough reason for them to worship or pay respects to it, seeking success, protection, good luck, and so on, revealing a truly pick 'n' mix spiritual mentality. So deeply ingrained is the idolatrous mindset, taught, and passed on down from generation to generation.

To illustrate this tendency, my friend sent me some photos via e-mail, dated 2006, of a large figure of Mickey Mouse, about seven feet tall and wearing headphones, which was standing outside a fashionable coffee house in central Bangkok. Well, that's not so unusual, you might think—nice for the kids. However, what *is* unusual is that, on closer inspection, Mickey Mouse, too, is garlanded with flowers around his neck! There are lit candles at his feet and some Thai people, plus a few westerners, are reverentially "paying respects" and offering incense to what had obviously become "the Mickey Mouse god"! This may sound bizarre but, sadly, it is true. I'm told that this idol is no longer there but it looks from the photos as if there was some serious worship going on back then.

I share these things not to shame anyone but to try to understand the underlying spiritual principles of what is actually going on here. Whether placing offerings at Queen Victoria's statue or at Mickey Mouse's feet, this behavior is clearly idolatrous. So, let's take a closer look to see what idolatry actually is.

There are many ways of describing it but here is a simple definition that I like and will have in mind when I refer to idolatry:

"Idol worship is revering [or worshiping] anything other than God."[2]

This includes any created thing (such as a person, stone, or tree) as well as anything that comes forth from something or someone created (such as an idea or a philosophy), all of which is not God, rather than the Creator of all things, who is God.

I am not suggesting here that created things are not to be respected or are bad—God himself said after he had made everything, that "it was very good" (Gen 1:31). What is crucial, though, is our right relationship to them. As God is their (and our) Maker, he is the only one truly worthy of our worship. He must take the central place in our lives—be "on the throne of our hearts," as it were—above anything or anyone else. We can then respect other people and things recognizing that God is their Source and Creator and so avoiding falling into idolizing or worshiping them. To do that would be to give our loyalty and devotion in an inappropriate way and where they are simply not due.

Here's an illustration. Suppose you had a friend called George who had worked hard to get a university degree and had done really well, but on the day when the degrees were being given out, the principal gave George's not to him, in reward for all his hard work, but to someone else altogether who has not done a thing. All the honor and recognition go to quite the wrong person. This is totally inappropriate and for George is a shocking disappointment. You can imagine how strongly he feels about it!

This to me is a clear picture of the nature of idolatry. God, who has done all the work and deserves our worship, honor and recognition, doesn't get them. Something or someone else, that he has created and which is completely undeserving, receives them instead. No wonder God abhors idolatry (Deut 32:16–22).

At its core, I would say that idolatry is a declension from "the norm": it perverts our relationship to creation as God intended it to be, which in its essence is pure and good.

You may wonder, then: Is Buddhism a form of idolatry? For those who have a knowledge of Buddhism, it may be easy to think it is not, as in

2. Beale, *We Become What We Worship*, 133, emphasis mine.

the original teachings, Buddha never asked his disciples to worship him. He only claimed to point the way that, he taught, each must find for themselves. However, we need to look at the origin of Buddha's teaching and his spiritual goal more closely to see whether Buddhism is actually idolatry.

This was one of the significant insights I had as a Buddhist nun, when I came to know God in the temple. I saw that Buddha himself only ever claimed to be a human being, and I asked myself: Why do I give myself to the teaching of a man, a part of creation, when I can worship the Creator of that man and of everything, who is God? However brilliant and subtle Buddha's teaching had appeared, such "wisdom," which the Bible describes as: "not [descending] from above, but is earthly, sensual, demonic" (Jas 3:15 nkjv) now seemed meaningless and insignificant compared to the knowledge and worship of the one true God, his Creator, whose wisdom is from above (Jas 3:17).

From my experience of Buddhism, as it is a philosophy that comes forth from a man, from a part of creation, I would say that without question it is idolatrous. And indeed, even though Buddha did not desire to be worshiped, Buddha statues, Buddha's bone relics, and so on, have over the years become, for many Asian Buddhists, more than just a reminder of a teacher and what he taught: they have become actual objects of veneration—idols in themselves.

As we have seen, animism, witchcraft, and the occult can all "sit" well with folk Buddhism. So, are these, too, forms of idolatry? Dr. Jonathan Burnside describes witchcraft (which he considers to be the same as the occult) clearly in this regard:

> "Witchcraft expresses our desire to carve out a space where we can make things happen apart from God . . . the manipulation of spiritual powers for our own ends is a form of human pride, which seeks to replace God with ourselves . . . This is why witchcraft is explicitly presented in the Bible as a form of idolatry."[3]

From what we have seen already, an interesting question arises: Why would so many Buddhists have a strong propensity to embrace such a variety of idolatrous spiritual practices? This is something that I have seen in my own life in the past, as well as what we find in Thailand.

---

3. Burnside, "Covert Power: Unmasking the World of Witchcraft," 5.

In trying to understand this complex matter, I've noticed that an important aspect of the nature of idolatry is that, once it has been engaged with in some form or other, it's as if a door is opened to the potential of worshiping a multitude of other created things. Idolatry tends toward being "not fussy" by nature, where the "familial likeness" of the idols seems to attract one another. In this way, idolatry is often seen as the worship of many gods/idols rather than the one, true God.

This doesn't mean that all idolaters will worship anything indiscriminately—some can be quite particular—but once having engaged with idolatry in some form or other, certainly brings with it the *potential* to worship or seek help from other created things, too. This helps to explain why a Thai folk Buddhist might want to give offerings to a statue of a queen, even a foreign one.

From what I noticed, Buddhism generally proves ineffective in protecting its followers from practicing other forms of idolatry. My understanding here is that because Buddhism is a form of idolatry, it easily accommodates other kinds, too.

Once someone has stepped through the door of idolatry, through whichever way, the possibilities can then become manifold, where individuals themselves may be amazed at what they are capable of worshiping, as I am now as I look back.

One afternoon, during my early years as a Buddhist before I was ordained, I was in great emotional turmoil, and in desperation I found myself spontaneously asking for help from a tree. Even though I had never done that before (or since!), not knowing God then, it felt perfectly natural to me, to look for help in time of need to something created, something tangible. As I think back now, it seems as futile as worshiping "the Mickey Mouse god"! But at the time, it was very real to me. It was yet another thing I have needed to repent of since becoming a Christian.

As Andrew Comiskey explains clearly: "We're vulnerable to all kinds of idolatry when our primary desire is not worshipping the Creator."[4]

Regardless of our nationality or where we live, idolatry is something anyone can be vulnerable to. We have an abundance of idols in the West: brands, celebrities, food, money, and so on. Idols of the East and the West may or may not be the same—there has been much interchange in the last

4. Comiskey, *Pursuing Sexual Wholeness*, 53.

few decades—but the range of possibilities for us to be held captive by idols fashioned with our hands, hearts, and minds is enormous. I think we can say it is as vast as the variety of created things and all that issues out of them—which gives us ample scope! (Please see the list of different types of idolatry in "Exploring Further 6" on page 127 for further examples of what can become idols for us.)

> "The Lord your God is God of gods and Lord of lords, the great God." (Deut 10:17)

How does God feel about idolatry? These scripture verses set in the heart of the Ten Commandments, given to us directly by God through Moses and written into the very fabric of the Christian faith, helps us to know God's heart toward idolatry and what he expects of his people:

> "You shall have no other gods before Me. You shall not make for yourself a carved image—any likeness *of anything* that is in heaven above, or that is in the earth beneath, or that is in the water under the earth; you shall not bow down to them nor serve them. *For I, the Lord your God, am a jealous God.*" (Exod 20:3–5a nkjv, emphasis mine)

Even if the idol gods of the Old Testament are different to ours today (some are still the same), the spiritual principles regarding idolatry have not changed. Here we clearly have God's instructions not to make, worship, or turn to any idol or image of any part of creation (the words translated "image" and "likeness" are also used for idols in different places in the Old Testament). Elsewhere, we are told not even to mention their names (Exod 23:13b) or show any interest in them at all (Deut 12:30), nor to marry anyone who worships idols (Deut 7:1–6). Idolatry is often condemned by the prophets, too (e.g., Jer 7:30–31).

It is interesting to note that God did not want his people to make any image or form even of him. Apart from the fact that no human effort could ever represent God accurately (Isa 40:18), this maintains a clear distinction between the Creator and (his) creation, and between the Creator and the idol gods (Deut 4:15–20). We, too, need to keep very clear about this distinction.

God told Moses explicitly what to do, from the time when the Israelites first went in to take the land of those who worshiped idols:

"The images of their gods you are to burn in the fire. Do not covet the silver and gold on them, and do not take it for yourselves, or you will be ensnared by it, for it is detestable to the Lord your God. Do not bring a detestable thing into your house or you, like it, will be set apart for destruction. Regard it as vile and utterly detest it, for it is set apart for destruction." (Deut 7:25–26)

The message is unequivocal: flee from idolatry and worship God alone (Deut 6:5).

Sadly, despite these clear warnings, idolatry seems to have been God's people's main sin, from very early on. Sometimes it went so far that they even brought images and altars of idol gods into the temple, the house of the Lord God himself. Here, God was confused with other gods. Strange practices in accordance with the customs of the surrounding nations, from where such idol gods had been brought, were introduced into what was meant to be pure worship of God (2 Kgs 21:3–7; Jer 7:30).

When this "blending" of worship occurs, it is no longer idolatry; it has become *syncretism*—an ungodly mixture of truth and error, the merging of different beliefs and practices attempting spiritual union when they are clearly at variance with one another. Such "worship" is extremely displeasing to God. His people are supposedly entering into his holy presence but with their hearts and wills not conformed to his.

This syncretistic mix can still be found in Christians today. We are unlikely to take a wooden idol into church and bow down to it—most of us tend to sin more privately than that—but an example of such error would be a Christian who "merges" their beliefs thinking they can be a "Christian Buddhist."

Idolatry and syncretism are enemies of God in that they vie with him for our worship, loyalty, and attention. And it is very clear that he abhors them both (2 Kgs 23:1–25).

Some people may not think of God as having and/or expressing emotions, but he is a passionate God, and in Scripture he expresses strong feelings about idolatry:

"I was crushed by their adulterous heart which has departed from Me, and by their eyes which play the harlot after their idols." (Ezek 6:9b nkjv)

In biblical language, adultery and prostitution (Jer 3:1–3) are used as metaphors for Israel's (and our) idolatrous practices of turning from the living God to dead idols. Like a husband in pursuit of his unfaithful wife, God calls his people to change their adulterous ways.

As the psalmist writes:

> "They provoked Him to anger with their high places [where idols were worshiped], and moved Him to jealousy with their carved images." (Ps 78:58 nkjv)

We see God's attitude to idols expressed even through the meaning of the Hebrew words for them in Scripture. Here are a few examples (including some from GK Beale's insightful work on a biblical theology of idolatry):

"One word for idols . . . comes from a Hebrew root meaning "roll." The noun form can mean either 'pellets of dung' or 'shapeless, loggy things.' Either way, 'loggy' or 'dungy,' the word expresses the utmost contempt."[5]

"While such idols were highly valued by their worshipers, their real value was equal to excrement."[6]

"Little dung balls" was a particular favorite of the prophet Ezekiel that he used in reference to idol gods. In Scripture he is recorded using it about forty times!

Some other descriptions applied to idols include: "repulsive" (1 Kgs 15:13); "worthless" (2 Kgs 17:15); and the prophet Isaiah talks of them as "but wind and confusion" (Isa 41: 29b).

So, how does this apply to Christians today?

I have often wondered if idolatry is the biggest threat to the Christian life and faith. One Christian friend of mine suggests that it is God's primary "opponent" throughout Scripture, and we see that much of the Bible is taken up with it.

One thing is for sure: it does need to be clearly renounced and repented of.

> "I am the Lord, that is My name; and My glory I will not give to another, nor My praise to carved images." (Isa 42:8 nkjv)

5. Beale, *We Become What We Worship*, 307.
6. Ibid., 308.

In the next chapter there are some helpful suggestions on how Christians can deal with past idolatry (and immorality and the occult), but here I will take a quick look at how we can identify and deal with any current idolatry.

As *we* are now temples of the Holy Spirit, the primary place that we need to look for idols is not so much outside of ourselves—although they do need to be dealt with on that level, too—but inside, in our hearts and minds. It is really important for us to check from time to time if God is truly "number one" in our lives, as we see from Scripture he should be and longs to be.

We need to keep a careful watch. Idolatry can take place in many ways: gradually or very suddenly, deliberately or inadvertently. It may sound odd to say so, but missionaries to countries like Thailand need to be aware of the potential pull of any local idols, and if they start to feel any attraction to them—and it has happened—to humbly be willing to get help, confess, and renounce them.

We give idolatry access more readily through any areas in our lives that are unhealed and/or not totally given over to God yet. We may not *want* to have idols in our lives, we may hate them even; but our hearts are needy and where we don't look to God and his ways for our needs to be met we may be shocked at the ease with which we bow down or "bend into" to the created.

Sometimes, we are so comfortable with our idolatry we can easily be blind to it (or else we simply don't want to see it). We need the help of the Holy Spirit to reveal it to us clearly. Obviously, the cleaner our hearts and thoughts, the easier it will be to spot any idols coming in—a bit like seeing dirt in a clean room. When we do let idols settle in, an intense battle for our hearts, minds, and worship can ensue.

If we want to know if something or someone is an idol for us, we can simply ask: Are we in bondage to it/them? Do our lives fall apart when it/they are not there? Can we live without it/them? Is it or are they more important to us than God?

How do we know if we have idols as Christians? Here are a few important telltale signs to look for:

- Generally we start to feel lukewarm about being a Christian and start to lose interest in reading the Bible. More and more, our interest, time, energy, and money goes toward our idol(s).

- The image of our idol (whether it is a thing or a person) "takes up residence" in our imaginations and occupies our thoughts to some degree or other. In extremes of idolatry, it feels as if it is always there— it "becomes a part of us." For instance, when we try to read the Bible, something of that idol is there to distract us—even to the point that at times, we don't want to or are not able to read the Bible at all.

- Are we able to see the cross? As we look at it, we may find ourselves unable to see it clearly—or not at all—but we see the image of our idol there instead.

If these telltale signs, all or in part, are there then we need to make a choice: are we willing to renounce our idol(s)—to state clearly that we will give it up and no longer worship it? This can be very challenging. In extreme cases, where idolatry has really taken hold, we may even feel that we will "die" if we give it up—we can't imagine life without it. If we find ourselves in this position, we definitely need mature and sensitive Christian help and prayer.

To whatever degree of idolatry we are in, we need to face up to it and admit it, dealing with it clearly and resolutely. No one else can do that for us. (In "Exploring Further 4: there is a Prayer for Renouncing Buddhism, Idolatry and/or the Occult" on page 123—and see also "Exploring Further 7: a Prayer for the Confession of Relational Idolatry and/or Sexual Immorality" on page 129—that may be used for this.)

When you are spending time with your Buddhist friend—whichever group of Buddhists they belong to—it will be very helpful for you to be aware that Buddhism is a form of idolatry.

Pray for your friend to become aware of their idolatrous mindset. Pray that their strong desire to worship no longer goes toward the created, or something that has come forth from the created, but that their mind is freed to know for themselves the Creator of all, so that their worship is directed toward the rightful one.

Now we have had a brief look at idolatry, we will take a closer look at how idolatry, immorality, and the occult "sit" and function together.

Chapter 8

An Unholy Alliance

> "The acts of the flesh are obvious: *sexual immorality,* impurity and debauchery; *idolatry* and *witchcraft* ... selfish ambition ... drunkenness, orgies, and the like ... Those who live like this will not inherit the kingdom of God." (Gal 5:19–21, emphasis mine)

As we have seen, various forms of idolatry and the occult are often found together, so too, immorality is often found to be with them—forming an "unholy alliance." There are clear examples of this in the Bible: see 2 Kings 17:6–18 and 23:4–16.

I am very grateful for the following story to Grace, a missionary friend who works with Thai women in one of Bangkok's red-light districts, where she and her team seek to fulfill the calling of Isaiah 61:1–4: to release prisoners from darkness and bring them abundant life through Jesus.

This is a composite story, made up from various events Grace commonly witnesses. I accompanied Grace and her team one time into the bars and have personally witnessed much of what she writes here to be true. It gives a glimpse of the complexities that draw women into prostitution and make it so difficult for them to escape it.

> "Do not degrade your daughter by making her a prostitute, or the land will turn to prostitution and be filled with wickedness." (Lev 19:29)

The sun goes down early in Bangkok. As the shadows grow, the bright neon signs of the bars in the red-light area begin to seduce the vulnerable and broken into its trap. Ying jumps off the motorbike "taxi" into the plaza. Her mobile rings; she quickly answers it. It's her mom saying that her dad is in hospital and she wants money to be sent for his hospital fees. Ying tells her she'll call back later.

She is in a hurry but pauses to *wai* (make a slight bow with the palms of the hands pressed together, the polite Thai greeting) seeking good luck from the large statue of the four-faced Hindu god, Brahma. It sits pre-eminent on the sprawling shrine at the entrance to the bars which surround the plaza on all sides. This begins a familiar routine of idolatrous and occult worship before Ying will start to dance and sell her body through the night. She's a folk Buddhist, as are most of the women who work here and she is used to idols. As a child, she was dedicated to some in her village by her parents, who also taught her great fear and respect of these "sacred objects."

Entering the bar, she finds a corner and begins to put on her mask, layering make-up to hide her true identity and feelings. She slips into a string bikini, pins a number onto her top and pulls on her high boots.

She emerges to *wai* the idols on the shrine above the counter where alcohol is sold. It has been freshly attended to with the idols' "favored" drinks and little pieces of food. One of the prostitutes is offering lit incense and then takes down some of the idols food offerings and shares an idolatrous supper with the dancers—"a dark act of communion" affirming their allegiance to these gods.

Ying has fresh hope tonight of finding that one elusive rich foreign man who will commit to her and "make it all okay." How many men will pay for her services before she finds him, she wonders.

As night sets in, she takes down the phallic idol from the shrine. She dips it into a glass of alcohol and begins the ritual of "dedicating" the entrance, the tables, the dance stage and each of the women, including herself. All of them in turn "pay respects" to it after it touches them. What's left of the alcohol is ceremonially thrown outside the door of the bar, in the belief that this will help to draw in the men who are walking past.

For a few minutes, the night workers from the surrounding bars who are watching Ying turn their focus from work to ritual. The tourists who have come here to buy sex miss its significance and instead are amused, jumping aside to avoid the splash, oblivious to the fact that the ceremony with the phallic idol is aimed directly at them.

Feeling better prepared now, Ying climbs onto the stage perpetuating the sacrifice of Thailand's daughters.

Ying dropped out of school at fifteen, an acceptable age by government standards. Her farming parents were in debt and Ying's failed relationship with her high-school boyfriend had left her with a child and no means of support.

She believes it is her duty to make a sacrifice for her family—a sacrifice that, in Ying's mind, is justified by the hope that she will make a lot of money. Her limited understanding of Buddhism convinces her that this is her karma and she will make merit by fulfilling the duty she has to her parents in supporting them in this way. Even though it feels like she is buying her parents approval and acceptance, they certainly don't resist.

Ying has already made more money through prostitution than she ever knew was possible. She's aware, though, that dirty money easily slips through the hands that grasp it, and for all she earns, it's never enough.

Ying comes down off the stage, throws a thin shawl round her tiny waist, and grabs a quick drink. A man is interested but she has other concerns just now and so slips out of the door.

On the balcony, scantily dressed women sit on bar stools huddled around the fortune-teller who comes every night with her tarot cards. Business is always good; the prostitutes come desperate to know their destiny. Ying pushes her way in and asks what the outcome for her father will be. She's told that he will find health and also that soon she will find a rich foreign man. Ying smiles then she shares that she went to the temple that very afternoon to make a love potion to entice one. The fortune-teller confirms that she did the right thing. The prostitutes are familiar with witchcraft and use it quite often: love potions, covenants with spirits, sacred tattoos to name a few. Ying pays the woman and, much encouraged, hastens back to the bar.

> "Let no one be found among you . . . who practises divination or sorcery, interprets omens, engages in witchcraft, or casts spells, or who is a medium . . . who consults the dead." (Deut 18:10–11)

Ying dances, watching herself narcissistically in the mirror, captivated by her own beauty. She catches the eye of a foreign man and holds his gaze. The love potion, she feels, has chosen its victim. He's hooked. She begins to reel him in. Done. The *mama-san* (pimp) moves in to take his money to seal the deal.

Next morning, Ying wants to take the man to the temple. Still intoxicated and wanting to please her, he freely agrees to go and carries the offerings that she has prepared for the idols on a tray, walking behind her like a slave in tow. Most of the men who use her services are happy to go with her to the temple.

> "The men began to indulge in sexual immorality with Moabite women, who invited them to the sacrifices to their gods. The people ate the sacrificial meal and bowed down before these gods." (Num 25:1–2)

Lost in her charm, he follows Ying through the rituals, willingly wearing the amulets around his neck and "blessed" strings tied around his wrists; signs of being bound to her idol gods. After which she invites him to her home in the provinces.

She calls her parents then wires them some money. Her father is improving.

Ying takes the man to her small village—a completely different world hundreds of miles away from Bangkok, carrying the money, alcohol, and other gifts she insists he bring. On arrival, she feels a fleeting sense of success as she presents her "trophy" to her parents causing them to feel proud.

As the man sleeps, they perform rituals to the idols and spirits, seeking their "help" to keep him bound to them. They see him as key to building up their finances and status.

He is living out his fantasy—feeling dazed in this distant, exotic land, but a phone call from Europe is an abrupt wake-up call. He hurries outside so that no one will hear that his wife is waiting for his return and is anxious at the loss of communication. He knows they need to get back to Bangkok immediately.

Ying sees him off at Bangkok airport. As soon as she has gone, he changes into his business suit in the airport restroom and rids himself of the strings from his wrists. The amulets he hides in the inside pocket of his briefcase for his next trip.

While he's still in the air, Ying is back in the bar. She has already emailed him (along with those other men she calls "darling") to remind him of his commitment. She will wait for his phone calls and will check her bank account carefully for his promised monthly transfer. Only then can she be sure that the potion continues to work and she still has him hooked.

She downs some whisky and winces before climbing back onto the stage.

Grace explains a little of the background of those they work with:

"Most of our girls come from Isaan, the northeast part of Thailand. This area has much poverty, with many of the girls coming from under-privileged families. *The majority of Isaan people are folk Buddhist with witchcraft and idolatry clearly woven into their Buddhist beliefs.* (This part of Thailand is home to some of the country's most famous Buddhist monks and temples.)

"Whereas the Buddhist teaching of karma can leave people feeling powerless, witchcraft and idolatry *appear*, albeit falsely, to give them some degree of control over their often despairing lives.

"In the past in the northeast it was considered shameful—under-standably—to have a daughter in prostitution, but now disdain has turned to greed as many of the poor, having sat passively watching their neighbors get richer, no longer resist but 'take a bite of the cherry' themselves.

> "Woe to those who call evil good and good evil, who put darkness for light and light for darkness, who put bitter for sweet and sweet for bitter." (Isa 5:20)

"In giving their daughters to prostitution, they hope it will quench their lust for such things as a nice house, a pick-up truck, whisky parties and an endless supply of money. They 'console' themselves with the hope that, one day soon, she will find a rich foreign man, a symbol of prosperity, who will take care of them all."

Many Thai people hate the prostitution in their country and feel very ashamed of it, I hasten to add.

Grace's eye-opening story does raise many questions, though.

What enables some Thai people to give their children willingly into prostitution?

Why are there so many prostitutes—men, women, and children—in Thailand?

Why for some people groups, even when they are under the same pressures of poverty, would prostitution of any kind be unthinkable? Why would they rather die of hunger before such a thought would enter their minds?

Surely, even to be able to contemplate doing such a thing must have spiritual roots. There is a reason why some people are able to consider it as an option and others never ever could.

But what is it?

The polite explanation we often hear is: poverty and lack of education. And that seems reasonable enough. But it doesn't explain why for the other people groups in similar circumstances, prostitution is unthinkable.

Here is my understanding of it.

As we see from Ying's story, (folk) Buddhism, worshiping idols, and the occult are a fundamental part of her lifestyle. This toxic spiritual mixture is what many Thais, especially in the provinces, will have been born into. And, although it's not always easy to perceive, Scripture shows us that partaking of such a spiritual mixture draws people into ever increasing darkness and bondage (Pss 106:36, 39).

(For a brief look at the key part idolatry plays in the breakdown of morality, both sexually and otherwise, please see "Exploring Further 8: Romans 1: Explaining the Effects of Idolatry" on page 131.)

The answer lies in what is worshiped and believed—as summed up succinctly by the prophet Hosea, who found himself living in a similar mixture of idolatry and immorality: "[They] became as vile as the thing they loved" (Hos 9:10).

I see idolatry as being *at the root* of the problems above that we find in Thailand, where, surely, some of the most extreme forms of both idolatry and sexual immorality are to be found. These two are, without question, linked (see, for example, Exod 32:1–6, 1 Cor 10:7–8, and Rev 2:14). As Grace put it to me: "I have no doubt that idolatry and witchcraft are key enabling factors in deceiving and trapping families into prostitution."

It may be helpful here, having come across it (with the phallic idol) in Ying's story, to share a brief word about some of the gods of sexual idolatry.

Since ancient times, where God has not been known, some people have mistaken even our human procreative faculties to be the source and power of life itself and hence have worshiped them. Two well-known idol gods that represent this type of worship that we find mentioned in the Bible are Baal and Ashtoreth (the wife of Baal), with reference to Baal in Scripture made over sixty times.

Baal and Ashtoreth cults challenged the worship of God throughout much of Israelite history and were worshiped by the Israelites in times of apostasy (Judg 2:13). Baal was the god the prophet Elijah confronted (1 Kgs 18:19–40).

Leanne Payne deals most insightfully with this difficult subject:

> "When there is *worship* of the sun and moon, *of the created, sexual orgies always follow. We either worship the Creator or our own procreative faculties. Demons, principalities, and powers of the air attend this worship.* The dark inroads into human sexuality and personality from this activity are almost incomprehensible. This, of course, is what the Apostle Paul is referring to in Romans 1:23 and following."[1]

I would say that some of the rituals found in the prostitute bars *today* are rooted in "the worship of Baal," the very thing spoken against by the prophets of old.

(For more information on how the worship of Baal can even affect the church, and for the "Exploring Further 9: Prayer to Renounce Baal and Ashtoreth," please see page 133.)

"Flee from idolatry." (1 Cor 10:14)

Let's look further at idolatry, immorality and the occult working together.

I'd like to share the story of a close friend of our discipleship ministry in Thailand called Nong, a Thai Christian who came to us some years ago for help.

Before she became a Christian, Nong had been involved in numerous forms of idolatry. She was a practicing Buddhist who regularly visited Buddhist temples and was very attached to many Buddha statues, especially the ones she had inherited from her mother. She wore lots of Buddhist amulets around her neck, "for safety and protection." She worshiped other gods, too, and was also involved in the occult.

---

1. Payne, *The Healing Presence*, 233, emphasis mine.

She tells me she was vulnerable to idolizing people, sometimes having emotionally dependent and/or immoral relationships in which it was hard for her to set appropriate boundaries. Pop singers, TV, and movie stars easily became her idols, too.

Other things that became her idols included: her pet dogs (she felt devastated when they died), the television (she found it hard to switch it off even when she didn't have time to watch it), and work (losing all sense of time and even going to the office sometimes on holidays as she felt she had value when she worked).

When Nong first came to us as a Christian, she felt she was still a slave to many of these things.

Over a number of years, the Lord led her to give up her idols one by one—she told me that it would have been too overwhelming to give them all up at the same time. As she did so, she became increasingly free. Previously, although she had been a Christian for many years, Nong had never felt the love of God which she longed to do—her idols had been in the way. But as she gave them up, she was able to receive and feel God's love for the first time, having come into a much deeper and more authentic relationship with him. She was beginning to live in the freedom that came from worshiping the one true God alone with an undivided heart.

Nong has been on our discipleship ministry leadership team for some time now and is an exemplary member. She names and renounces her idols if she is tempted to worship them again, and is good at helping others to do the same. She tells me how much better she feels, and her shining countenance displays that to us all.

"If the Son sets you free, you will be free indeed." (John 8:36)

I have noticed, from ministry in Thailand and from my own life, that most of us who have (literally) worshiped idols will be particularly vulnerable to idolizing people, too. This applies to Christians as well as non-Christians.

In my early years as a Christian, if I inadvertently became too dependent on someone, say, a friend, and had fallen into emotional dependency, what I like to call relational idolatry (this occurred in my mind and heart, there was no outward sin), old Buddhist thoughts would start to bother me. At such times, I might have dreams that I was still a Buddhist nun and wake up feeling confused and unsettled, not knowing if I was a Buddhist or Christian. This was very odd, as usually I was completely sure I was a Christian.

Once when this happened, it became more extreme, and as the bondages of relational idolatry and Buddhism intensified, *I felt at times as if I was alone, lost in a deep void, where it became increasingly hard to find Jesus.* Not able to find the way out, I thank God for his provision of a mature and godly pastor, who knew how to help me.

He explained to me that having opened the door to relational idolatry I had opened the door to spiritual idolatry, too, making a way for old Buddhist thoughts and feelings to come back in. These two kinds of idolatry were working in tandem (Deut 28:15, 20, 28).

The only way out, he said, was to truly repent, meaning to turn completely away from the relational idolatry and from Buddhism (plus anything else that needed to be repented of) and to set appropriate boundaries immediately (for example, not to spend time with, or even see, the person concerned).

I repented immediately and did all that he advised, and peace and clarity returned as quickly as they had left.

This pastor had incredible insight to see what was going on and once I was out of it he warned me that as Buddhism had once had a strong hold over my mind, I had to be particularly careful what I did with my thought life. He told me to daily put on the helmet of salvation for the protection of my mind (Eph 6:17). This I did (and do!) willingly, as I knew I had to guard my mind and that any turning back to my "idol(s)" would put me in great danger once more.

I was interested to ask Nong if she had noticed this connection in her own life, and she said that she had.

As I had found out, there can be a great cost for our idolatrous disobedience. At that time, I had wrongly assumed that I could give "most" of myself to God, but keep something back for me. However, the part I held back from God then became the point of my undoing. But even with this more extreme experience I have described above, God used it for good. Once I realized that I couldn't hold anything back from God and assume I'd be safe, it became a very real and significant turning point in my Christian life.

No wonder we find this theme recurring throughout the Bible. Here quoted by Jesus, in what is now known as "the greatest commandment":

> "Hear, O Israel: the Lord our God, the Lord is one. Love the Lord your God with all your heart and with all your soul and with all your mind and with all your strength." (Mark 12:29b–30, emphasis mine)

This is so important, as it seems to me, that where we don't love God *with everything*, we will be worshiping idols or be in sin of some kind.

It's interesting to note that when I fell back into idolatry, even as a Christian, it led me to feel as if I was in a deep void.

As we have seen, I believe Buddhism to be a form of idolatry, and emptiness, we know, is the Buddhist goal; but is there a connection? *Does all idolatry lead to emptiness? Scripture implies that it does.* Here God is speaking to Jeremiah regarding Israel's falling into idolatry:

> "What injustice did your fathers find in Me, that they went far from Me and walked after emptiness [*worshiped idols*] and became empty?" (Jer 2:5 nasb, emphasis mine. See also Isa 44:9–10 and Jer 16:19.)

Emptiness, then I would say, is not some sublime spiritual goal but the inevitable consequence of idolatry.

As Peter Stuhlmacher further adds for us: "Whoever follows after that which is nothing [the idols], becomes nothing himself (Jeremiah 2:5)!"[2]

What we worship has powerful consequences. As G. K. Beale notes perceptively:

> "All human beings are imaging beings and are made to be committed to God and to reflect him, and if they don't, they will be committed to some part of the creation and reflect it."[3]

Scripture shows us clearly that we become what we worship. The following verses sum up idols and the consequences of worshiping them:

> "[They] are silver and gold, made by human hands. They have mouths, but cannot speak, eyes, but cannot see. They have ears,

---

2. From Peter Stuhlmacher, *Paul's Letter to the Romans*. Louisville: Westminster John Knox, 1994, 36. Quoted in Beale, *We Become What We Worship*, 211.

3. Ibid., 162.

but cannot hear, noses, but cannot smell. They have hands, but cannot feel, feet, but cannot walk, nor can they utter a sound with their throats. *Those who make them will be like them, and so will all who trust in them.*" (Pss 115:4–8, emphasis mine)

We have, in a sense, a way of becoming what we set our eyes and hearts upon. Simply put, if we worship idols we become like them; if we worship the true and living God as revealed in his Son Jesus, we become like him:

"And we, who with unveiled faces all reflect the Lord's glory, are being transformed into his likeness with ever-increasing glory, which comes from the Lord, who is the Spirit." (2 Cor 3:18 niv 1985 Edition)

I have noticed this to be true.

Some years ago, I was living on an island, about an hour by ferry from central Hong Kong, where our small outreach team had the task of taking Jesus to the people in our village—mainly Chinese grannies and grandpas. Many of them had made their living fishing, whereas many of the younger generation had left the island to find work in the city. We really enjoyed getting to know the villagers and helping when we could, for instance by taking them to the local hospital when they were unwell or visiting them in bad weather.

The majority were heavily into idol worship and had been for most of their lives, and I couldn't help noticing that many of them bore a "likeness" to their idols, often appearing somewhat grey and lifeless, as if there was a submerged veil over their faces (see 2 Cor 4:3).

As some of them came to know Jesus, there was a definite transformation in them as his life, joy, and peace filled their faces and their lives.

I remember vividly a Chinese man in Hong Kong who had worshiped a "monkey god" before becoming a Christian. Strange as it may sound, during a time of worshiping God with a group of other Christians, his body suddenly took on the appearance and manner of a monkey. He had taken on the likeness of his idol and the accompanying demonic forces he had previously given himself to. And now, as God was touching him, these effects that he had taken into himself from worshiping such a god, were surfacing so that he could begin to be released from them.

Likewise, Grace told me that as they were praying for one of her girls; she had seen her slithering across the floor like a snake.

When we worship some part of creation, we open ourselves up to spiritual darkness. Scripture shows us that behind the apparent impotence of the idols lurk real danger and the possibility of demonic oppression:

> "The sacrifices of pagans [to idols] are offered to demons, not to God, and I do not want you to be participants with demons. You cannot drink the cup of the Lord and the cup of demons too; you cannot have a part in both the Lord's table and the table of demons." (1 Cor 10:20–21)

As G. K. Beale notes: "Idols are one of the main instruments used by the forces of darkness to keep people in darkness."[4]

You can find a summary of some of the things discussed in the last two chapters in two tables which contrast the nature of idols and idolatry with the nature of God (see "Exploring Further 10" on page 135) and some important differences between what happens to idolaters and God's intent for Christians (see "Exploring Further 11" on page 137).

> "But if from there you seek the Lord your God, you will find him if you seek him with all your heart and with all your soul." (Deut 4:29)

I remember staying for the first time at a Christian friend's apartment in a nice suburb of Hong Kong. To my amazement, as soon as I entered it I spotted a reclining Burmese Buddha statue, about eighteen inches long, in the hall. Quite honestly, I was shocked. Later, I seized the opportunity to ask my friend politely if she knew what this statue was. She replied: "It's a prince." This was true, as Buddha came from a royal family, so I asked her: "Do you know it's a statue of Buddha?" She replied that she honestly didn't know. She then asked me, "What should I do?" and I replied: "You need to destroy it."

My friend was concerned, as it had cost a lot of money, but I said: "It's the only thing to do with it, as it is an idol."

After we had chatted for a while, I took my things to my room to give her some space to think. When I came back a short time later, I was so impressed—there she was, kneeling on the floor, determinedly trying to

4. Ibid., 265.

saw its head off! As it turned out, the wood was so hard she wasn't able to do it, so she took the easier option and threw it in the incinerator instead.

I was struck by my friend's commitment *not* to keep *any* idols. Her heart really was in the right place. Unintentionally she had welcomed one in, but once she realized what it really was, she had been prompt and decisive in dealing with it.

This, to me, is a picture of true repentance (Acts 26:20b).

This story reminds me of the decisive way in which the God fearing kings and prophets of the Old Testament dealt with idols found among God's people. Moses, for example, shows us here the way he dealt with the golden calf:

> "I took that sinful thing of yours, the calf you had made, and burned it in the fire. Then I crushed it and ground it to powder as fine as dust and threw the dust into a stream that flowed down the mountain." (Deut 9:21)

In 2 Kings 10:27 we read of the temple of Baal that ended up being used as a latrine! Here we see no sympathy with idols!

> "Dear friends, let us purify ourselves from everything that contaminates body and spirit, perfecting holiness out of reverence for God." (2 Cor 7:1)

We saw in the previous chapter how Christians can identify and repent of any *present* idolatry we may have. But it is necessary also to repent of and renounce all *past* idolatry and sin, too. The earlier this is done in our Christian lives, the better, for it plays a big part in the cure and restoration to the spiritual decline as described in Romans 1. The following story illustrates its importance:

Once when I was in Hong Kong, a Chinese Christian friend came to me looking very distressed. It was obvious she felt really bad, as if she was under a cloud of confusion and oppression. I asked her if she had specifically renounced the idols that she used to worship. She said, "No, not all of them." I suggested that this might be what was troubling her. As she was ready and willing to go ahead, I asked another friend to join us and we prayed for her, there and then.

We asked the Lord to show her what idols she needed to repent of. She then renounced each idol by name and asked Jesus to break the power it still had over her life. As she had previously been seriously into idol worship and the occult, it was a long prayer session! By the end though, the cloud had lifted, her countenance had changed, and her peace was restored. Thank you Jesus!

> "The blood of Jesus . . . purifies us from all sin. . . . If we confess our sins, he is faithful and just and will forgive us our sins and purify us from all unrighteousness." (1 John 1:7b, 9)

In light of the connection between spiritual and relational idolatry (as seen in Nong's story and mine above), I consider it to be important to name, repent of, and renounce any idols or gods we have worshiped (spiritually), and anything of the occult we have practiced, as well as the people and/or behaviors we have been (or still are) in bondage to. *Renouncing one without the other can keep us weak.* You may use the prayer for renouncing Buddhism, idolatry, and/or the occult in "Exploring Further 4" on page 123 as well as the prayer for the confession of relational idolatry and/or sexual immorality in "Exploring Further 7" on page 129.

In addition to this, it is important to note that we may be vulnerable in the same areas of sin and bondage that oppressed our ancestors. For this, it will help tremendously in bringing us greater freedom and healing if we repent of and renounce the idol gods and sins of former generations in our family. This is all quite biblical—as God said to Gideon:

> "Tear down your father's altar to Baal and cut down the Asherah pole beside it. Then build a proper kind of altar to the Lord your God." (Judg 6:25b–26a)

For instance, if our parents, grandparents, or great-grandparents were involved in idolatry, the occult, or immorality, we can name those things and bring them to the Lord Jesus in prayer, asking him to wash and cleanse us from any influence they may have had over our lives. Where the same sin has been conceived in us—for example, our father was an alcoholic or adulterer and we have that same tendency—that, too, needs to be owned and confessed by us.

Usually we do not confess and repent of the sins of other people, for each individual needs to be responsible to God for themselves. However, it is evident that particular types of sins can be "passed down" the family line, and hence the need to repent of and renounce them for the former generations of our families. (Please see "Exploring Further 12: Prayer for Breaking Generational Ties" on page 139.)

Truly, *even* today we can become free from idolatry, the occult, and immorality through Jesus Christ and be able to set our gaze unhindered upon God. *Jesus died for us to have such freedom* (John 8:36), *but we have to want it and pursue it humbly but doggedly.*

Some people, when they come out of Buddhism, experience an instant break from it, which is how it was with me. Once I came to Christ, I no longer wanted any involvement with Buddhism—Buddha statues, books, teaching, chanting, etc. If I do have Buddhist material now, it's only for use in writing books such as this and certainly not out of any lingering attachment to Buddhism.

Even so, it was still necessary for me to repent of and renounce my involvement with Buddhism (and all other idolatry, occult practices, and immorality) in Jesus' name.

With other former Buddhists, it may take time to explain why they can't keep their idols, Buddhist books, former meditation practices, and so on.

Once, I met a Western man, a former Buddhist, who was very attached to his Buddhist books. He asked me if it was okay to keep them now that he was a Christian. As soon as I explained that he needed to give them up and renounce any connection he still had with Buddhism, including all his books, he got rid of them. He just needed to know what to do.

It's not only books but any physical objects connected with past involvement in idolatry or the occult—idols, amulets, charms, and so on—that need to be given up and destroyed. As we read in Scripture:

> "Many who had believed came confessing and telling their deeds. Also, many of those who had practiced magic brought their books together and burned them in the sight of all. And they counted up the value of them, and it totaled fifty thousand pieces of silver." (Acts 19:18–19 nkjv)

We will have little hope of growing and maturing as Christians unless all this is dealt with decisively.

Regarding confession of sin in general, it is interesting that in our discipleship ministry in Thailand, we have found it unusually common for Thai Christians to have a complacent attitude toward sin, both sexual and otherwise. *I have often heard it said: "God is lovely, he forgives me my sin"— but said in a way that implies that the one saying it feels they have a right to carry on sinning, with no intention of stopping!*

It's true, God will forgive us our sin, but we are called to turn away from it and live holy lives (1 Pet 1:16).

This attitude among Thai Christians reveals, I feel, that their Buddhist mindset has not yet been clearly renounced. Buddhists do not think in terms of sin against a holy God, but of karma. They believe that they alone bear the consequences of their "good" and "bad" actions and that if they do enough good things it will outweigh the bad. When they come to know Jesus, if they continue to think in this way, it tends to produce very "busy" Christians, and it can easily dull their consciences to the need to live in obedience to God. (Interestingly, the apostle Paul faced a similar problem, which he wrote of in Romans 6:1–14.)

It's important to pray that the Holy Spirit of truth will help them have a clear conviction of sin, God's righteousness, and judgment (John 16:8). I often pray that people caught in this kind of thinking, will come to see their sin and hate it as God does. I am always delighted to see a Thai Christian—or any Christian for that matter!—who is truly convicted of their sin.

Although Thai Theravāda Buddhism does have a precept for lay Buddhists "not to commit adultery," its application can be vague and ineffectual. As a lay Buddhist for six years, I felt I was at liberty to interpret it in my own way—and many lay Buddhists it seems feel the same (i.e., to be faithful to the person you are with at the time, for however short a period that may be!). In that regard, it does not necessarily protect the Buddhist lay believer from sexual immorality.

How does this help you in understanding and reaching your Buddhist friend?

If they don't know Christ yet, check discreetly what type of Buddhist they are (i.e., which tradition they follow) and how committed to it they feel. It would be helpful to know if they are involved in other forms of idolatry and/or occult practices. Please exercise sensitivity when asking about this.

> Prayer: *Dear Lord Jesus, please open my Buddhist friend's spiritual eyes so that they can see you and in your presence will be able to see idolatry, the occult, and immorality as the defiling and dangerous things they are and willingly turn away from them. In Jesus' name I pray. Amen.*

The wonderful thing is that God created and loves every Buddhist on this earth and desires to win each one back to himself. There may well be a part God wants you to play in this, as we shall see in the next chapter on evangelizing Buddhists.

Chapter 9

Evangelizing Buddhists

"I am not ashamed of the gospel, because it is the power of God that brings salvation to everyone who believes." (Rom 1:16)

"Have no fear of them, nor be troubled, but in your hearts reverence Christ as Lord. Always be prepared to make a defense to anyone who calls you to account for the hope that is in you, yet do it with gentleness and reverence; and keep your conscience clear." (1 Pet 3:14–16a rsv)

Some time ago, I heard Jackie Pullinger say that she thought idol worshipers were wonderful. I thought: *How are you going to explain that, Jackie?* She went on to say: "The reason they're wonderful is because they're looking, it's just that they haven't heard the name of Jesus yet!"

It may be worth considering, just for a moment, why we bother to share Jesus with Buddhists (or anyone else, for that matter). The answer is quite simple: Jesus is unique, and he has supremacy (Col 1:18). He is high above all other gods and human philosophies (Col 2:8). He is God's beloved Son (Col 1:13), the true (1 John 5:20) and living God (Rev 1:18), the exact revelation and representation of the Father (Col 1:15), in whom dwells the totality of divine attributes and power (Col 1:19; 2:9). He is the Creator and Sustainer of the universe as well as its goal (Col 1:16–17) and the only name by which we can be saved (Acts 4:12).

God has given me a real love for Buddhists, as well as a confidence that if he can draw me to himself, he can draw other Buddhists, too. I have been greatly blessed to see this happen in many places in the world, from a Western Buddhist monk to a whole family of Tibetan Buddhists in Mongolia, as well as many Thai people.

We who know Jesus are his ambassadors (2 Cor 5:20), at times used by God to help to call others to him. When I was a Buddhist nun and I saw the video of Jackie Pullinger and the brothers and sisters in Hong Kong, God used *them* to call me out of Buddhism and show me Jesus.

I have already shared some thoughts on how you can reach out to your Buddhist friend, but I want to write a little more, specifically on sharing Jesus with them.

Although Buddhists often appear to be amiable and approachable, evangelizing them has *not* proved to be easy, in either the East or the West. For instance, historically it has been a challenge in Thailand for Buddhists to come to know Jesus and stay strong in their Christian faith. This is evident from the fact that, after more than two hundred years of missionary presence there, the population is still only 1 percent Christian. I am glad to say that recently more Buddhists have been coming to faith in Jesus in Thailand, but there is still a long way to go.

So, how to do it?

There are many different strategies and approaches to evangelizing Buddhists, from big evangelistic rallies to Christians spending time alone with a Buddhist friend.

Some theologians and missionaries, I have noticed, look for a set method or formula to use—over which even some of our finest can disagree! Personally, I have found no particular method or formula apart from seeking God through prayer for each occasion and following the leading and prompting of his Holy Spirit. For this, an intimate relationship with God is key in enabling us to discern what he would have us do in each situation—what part we are to play.

Some Christians look for a "bridge" between Christianity and Buddhism, as if there is a neutral place where the two can meet and happily sit together. Although some concepts in Christianity and Buddhism may *appear* to be similar, being founded and rooted in different spiritual kingdoms,

I have found no *genuine* similarities between them. However, I would say that it is very important to build bridges of friendship and patiently spend time with your Buddhist friend as God leads you.

I would like to share with you some things I have found helpful and some I have not.

First, what has *not* worked?

Having come out of Buddhism so clearly, I was overly eager at first to share Jesus with my Buddhist friends, and I started off badly, more like a bull in a china shop!

Shortly after I left the temple, a close lay Buddhist friend came to visit me, travelling quite a way to see me. As she was telling me about the Buddhist meditation retreat she had been on—the kind of thing we would often chat about when I was a nun—I was itching for an opportunity to tell her how misguided she was. As soon as she finished talking, I told her quite directly and robustly that she was going to hell! She left soon after, somewhat bewildered, and not surprisingly, never attempted to contact me again.

On another occasion in those early years, I went back to see the Buddhist nuns. It's only for the purpose of evangelism (or funerals; most cremations in Thailand, even for Christians, take place in Buddhist temples) now that I visit temples—I know of a British Christian woman who went into some idol temples in Hong Kong for no other purpose than for sightseeing. Friends tell me it was a definite contributing factor in her losing her Christian faith; it simply faded away soon after.

The nuns, who I had known and lived with for so long, were really happy to see me, and that was great. They knew why I had disrobed and, I suspect, why I had gone to visit them. Before long though, we started to get lost in philosophical debate. Everyone behaved well, I should say, but the discussion became increasingly tense and heated. I guess they all felt drained afterwards—I certainly did!

On reflection, I can see that I rose to the bait. As Buddhism is a subtle, complex, and intellectual philosophy (Col 2:8), many of those who are serious about it are often more comfortable with intellectual discussions. Obviously, there can be a place for that; but being sucked into an argument, and engaging only on that level, I have found can waste a lot of time—going round and round in circles and ending up where you started. There needs to be more.

I was easily tempted back then to argue with Buddhists, but I have since learned to try to avoid this as it just gets people on the defensive. Tempers can become frayed, and at times, things can even turn quite ugly! I have found that it is far more effective to prayerfully wait for the Lord to give an opportunity for you to share and to talk in an unthreatening, matter-of-fact way. We need to let God work in other people by his Holy Spirit, not hammer them with our own arguments however sincere they may be.

Here are some steps I've found helpful that I recommend to you. They are condensed from visits that I've made to Buddhist temples over the years, for the purpose of sharing Jesus. They can also be used (adapted if necessary) in other contexts, too—if you are spending time with a Buddhist friend or relative, for example, or when spending time with someone involved in idolatry or a cult. For a summary of these preparations and procedure in evangelizing Buddhists, please see "Exploring Further 13" on page 141.

PREPARE YOURSELF

It's really important for this kind of ministry that we have confessed any sin and are right with God. Carrying (unconfessed) sin makes us feel unclean and unworthy, which serves to disempower us. If there are still strong patterns of binding sin in our lives, then it is not the time to think about this kind of outreach before first seeking the help and the freedom we need. It's important also that we check our hearts for any kind of idolatry, however gross or subtle. The freer we are from idolatry in our own lives, the more effective ministry to idolaters will be, and the safer. If you find any, confess it to a trusted friend and renounce it sometime before going.

Aim to be a "living letter" of the Christian message, one in which it is easy for others to see Jesus in us.

It's also important to "put on the full armor of God" (Eph 6:11–17) for our protection: the belt of truth, the breastplate of righteousness, the sandals of the gospel of peace, the shield of faith, the helmet of salvation, and the sword of the Spirit.

Failing to make the appropriate preparations can leave us vulnerable to confusion, deception, and bondage ourselves.

DON'T GO ALONE

It's preferable when evangelizing Buddhists of any kind not to go alone. Jesus sent people out in pairs (Mark 6:7). This may not always be possible, of course, but if it is, pray about which Christian friend(s) to invite. Some may be very keen, others may not; take the ones who show a genuine interest to go.

For visits to Buddhist temples, it is good to take mature Christians, as less mature believers may actually become intrigued by Buddhism and get drawn into it. I have seen this happen—someone who came with me asked the Buddhist nuns a lot of questions, obviously becoming increasingly interested in Buddhism while sharing nothing of their own faith!

PREPARE THE TEAM

Once you have the team, it's good if possible to meet together once or twice before the visit to pray. Together you can seek God for his timing (Exod 33:15) and strategy and ask him to speak to you through words, pictures, or scriptures, jotting down what you receive. Your prayers might include (if visiting a temple, for example) that God would lead you to those Buddhists that he wants you to meet, that he would go ahead by his Holy Spirit to prepare their hearts so that they are open to Jesus, and that he would give you his wisdom and discernment to know what to say to them.

This is also a good time to sketch out briefly what you and your team can expect and how you can support each other when you are in the temple.

ASK SOME FRIENDS TO PRAY FOR YOU

If possible, it is really supportive to have some Christian friends praying for you, at home or elsewhere, during the time you are visiting Buddhists. To have others seeking God for your team and the people you meet is really powerful and does change things. And please don't forget to let these friends know how the visit went once you get back. Sharing together can be a source of great encouragement and an opportunity to see the faithfulness of God at work.

TIME TO GO!

Once your preparations are made, it is time to go. It's good to be aware of Buddhist temple etiquette (without falling into idolatry!) and to remember that you are their guests. I have found it most helpful and would encourage you also to keep your eyes fixed on Jesus rather than dwelling on any images or idols you see and to remain prayerful (Eph 6:18a).

When we go to share the truth of Christ with Buddhists, it is helpful to be aware that "our struggle is not against flesh and blood, but against the rulers, against the authorities, against the powers of this dark world and against the spiritual forces of evil in the heavenly realms" (Eph 6:12).

Jesus has a real enemy who wants to keep Buddhists blinded to the truth. Sharing Jesus with them can be a "battle," often in the unseen places although sometimes we see evidence of it on earth, too. However, we are told not to be afraid (Josh 1:9)—the battle belongs to Jesus (Col 2:15). We don't fight in our own strength, but pray for Jesus and his holy angels to fight for us and protect us.

When one of your team gets into conversation with a Buddhist, it is important that the other(s) are supporting them silently in prayer as they speak. Be careful not to become distracted but stay focused. The one in conversation, too, can be silently praying, i.e., "Lord Jesus, please give me your words to say."

There have been times I've spent with a Buddhist monk or nun when they have started talking a lot about Buddhism. I then pray for an opening to share about Jesus.

One time it happened was when a Christian friend and I were visiting a temple in the provinces in Thailand. We met a Western nun I knew and as we talked to her she soon started teaching us Buddhism.

I prayed silently and before long the Lord impressed on me that we should offer to pray for her. So, I gently interrupted and said, "Can we pray for you?" and she said: "Yes."

When God prompts you to do something, his authority is with you, too.

My friend and I drew close to her and I prayed a simple prayer that the Lord Jesus would come and touch her and enable her to see and know him, to realize how much he loved her and how special she was to him.

As soon as I had finished, she shared with us that, even though she had been a Buddhist nun for more than twelve years, she couldn't say for sure that she had found the truth. Such a turnaround; from teaching us about Buddhism to real heartfelt vulnerability! Needless to say, we left elated.

As we just read, it's important to stay attentive to God's promptings to offer to pray for Buddhists—it provides a great opportunity for them to experience for themselves God's presence and touch.

Some temple visits I have made have been far less dramatic. Once, for instance, all the monks and nuns had gone on a silent retreat, unknown to us, and so we met no one. That's okay, too—we just prayed and trusted that our time there was not wasted.

SHARING JESUS WITH A BUDDHIST

It's very important, I have found, when you spend time with a Buddhist, that they hear the simple gospel message, as the opportunity arises. This is because they do not yet know Jesus personally or who he truly is. Some Buddhists may acknowledge him as a wise man or a prophet, but they are unable to recognize him as the Son of Man (Matt 8:20) and Son of God (John 1:49). There is a profound difference. When you share the gospel message with them, you are giving them the opportunity to hear—or hear afresh—the truth of who Jesus is. I believe that this played a significant part in the Western Buddhist monk Paul coming to know Jesus, as written in *I Once Was a Buddhist Nun*.[1]

Another occasion where I witnessed the importance of this was in 1996 when Jackie Pullinger encouraged some friends and I to spend a month helping members of a German church who were on long-term mission in Mongolia. We were based in a small town called Hinti, twelve hours by bus east of the capital, Ulan Bator. On most days, we were sent out in five or six teams of three or four people, including a Mongolian translator. We had the joy of taking food and clothes to the poor as well as sharing the simple gospel message with them (Jas 2:26). Some of those we met were Tibetan Buddhists.

What we witnessed in our various teams was amazing. It was here that God graced me to see a whole family of Buddhists come to Christ; they were so hungry to know him! Actually, many whole families came

1. Baker, *I Once was a Buddhist Nun*, 118.

to believe in him, day after day, as our little teams went out, often with miracles of healing and the baptism of the Holy Spirit, too.

When you are sharing the gospel message, it is best to wait patiently for God's timing, rather than blurt it out compulsively. If you share in the God-given moment, those listening will be more likely to receive it, or at least to be quiet long enough to be able to hear it! (Please see "Exploring Further 2: The Simple Gospel Message" on page 120.)

Each occasion is different, but there may be times when an opportunity arises to share Scripture with Buddhists. This will be helpful as "faith comes by hearing, and hearing by the word of God" (Rom 10:17 nkjv).

At my Thai church in central Bangkok, many of our members bring their Buddhist friends along each Sunday. My Thai pastor enjoys preaching the word of God and his sermons are filled with scriptures. Over the last few years, as he has invited non-believers to accept Christ at the end of each service, most weeks there have been Thai Buddhists becoming Christians.

Coming to know God is a very personal experience. Someone can talk about it as much as they like, but if it hasn't happened to you it can make quite frustrating listening. There are times when I see a Buddhist interested or even hungry to know God and so, as they like to discover things for themselves, there is a short, non-committal prayer that I suggest they pray, as the following story illustrates.

Once in Bangkok, a senior Thai Buddhist monk came to see me. It soon became clear he was really doubting Buddhism and this was obviously troubling him deeply.

A very learned man with a bright mind, he was trying hard to find answers through his intellect. I could see that he was becoming more and more confused and anxious as theories and ideas from different religions started spinning around in his head—a confusion that reminded me of my own mental state when I was coming out of Buddhism. He was desperate to know which of them was the truth!

He was keen to know why I had disrobed, so I shared my story with him. I was encouraged to see he could obviously relate to much of what I was saying.

Then I said to him: "Truth is conceived in your spirit, not in your mind. It is processed and understood in your mind but not conceived there. So, if you want to know if God is real, you can't 'think it out'—that's like a dog trying to catch its tail. Just pray: 'God, if you're real, I want to know you.' Then, one way or the other, you will find out for yourself."

This happens to be a very "dangerous" prayer—the type God loves to answer! I prayed it as a Buddhist nun one night, following the recommendation of a Christian friend, when I was muddled and fearful—and not long afterwards I disrobed!

I didn't hear the full outcome of this story, but soon after I was delighted to find out that this monk too had disrobed.

Jesus said: "Ask and it will be given to you; seek and you will find; knock and the door will be opened to you" (Matt 7:7).

When I have shared about Jesus with Buddhists, I've seen a whole range of reactions, from interest to indifference to antagonism, even. Although Buddhists tend to be gentle souls, I've often seen them "wriggling" to escape hearing the truth of salvation through Jesus, drawing on everything they have, it seems, in order to deny it. Some begin to "rattle" as they hear the gospel, suddenly becoming angry.

I can remember this happening to me when listening to Christians as a Buddhist nun. At times I reacted strongly, thinking: *I can't listen to you any more. I've just got to go!* And I would be gone!

If this happens, don't worry, keep cool—it's a sure sign that God is at work. As I share about Jesus now, I certainly don't go out deliberately to provoke people, but if I see this kind of response I get really excited, thinking: *Now God's moving!*

So, don't be concerned if people get angry or upset: it's (probably) not you they are reacting to but what Jesus has done on the cross! He is an offense to them spiritually, threatening the lies, deception, and darkness they are presently held by. We see strong reactions to Jesus in the Bible, too (Matt 8:29; Mark 1:24; 5:7).

AFTER LEAVING THE TEMPLE

Soon after leaving the temple, pray for Jesus to cleanse your minds, bodies, souls, and spirits with his blood. Pray, too for his protection, especially over your loved ones and your possessions. Check that everyone on your team is feeling okay, and ask if anything is bothering them.

FEEDBACK AND PRAYER

If possible, have a time of feedback and prayer together soon after your visit to the temple. Each person can share how their experience was. How did the prayer time that you (may have) had with your team before the visit match up with the visit? Were there words, pictures, or scriptures that matched from that prayer time together with what actually happened? It is good to spend some time thanking God for what he has done and for his faithfulness.

KEEP PRAYING FOR THE BUDDHISTS YOU MET AND SHARED JESUS WITH

We continued to pray for Paul the Buddhist monk after we met him, and he came to know Jesus six months later.

You might be wondering whether you need some special qualifications (such as having studied other religions at Bible college) or a particular understanding of Buddhism before you can share Jesus with Buddhists. If you do know something about Buddhism, that's good; but if you don't, this story may be an encouragement to you.

Some years ago, while living in Hong Kong, I went on a short-term mission trip to Thailand with an English friend. We were going to meet quite a few Buddhists and she was concerned because she didn't know much about Buddhism. However, a Chinese brother from our church prayed over her before we left and told her: "You know Christ and that is enough." And that was who she kept bringing. In fact, I was so impressed watching her share her faith with a Buddhist nun because she talked only of Jesus, and it was evident how clear her message about him was.

I can't help but feel that the Lord loves it when we reach out to Buddhists as he leads us. On one occasion we experienced an extraordinary miracle.

A couple of weeks before our visit to the temple where I used to live, I was praying with two English friends who had never been to a Buddhist temple before. We received pictures and encouragement from the Lord, as well as two scriptures: Ps 121:4 and 1 Cor 2:9.

On the day of the visit, as we met up to go, the friend who was going to drive the car was concerned. "There's a problem with one of the back tires," she said. "It's nearly flat."

I had a look and saw there was indeed a problem, but after discussing the situation, we all felt we should still go. As time was short, we prayed, pumped up the tire, and off we went, stopping a few times on the way to check it.

We arrived at the temple safely—but as I got out of the car, I heard a distinct hiss and noticed that the back tire was slowly going down.

Oh dear, we've got a puncture, I thought. *We don't want to get stuck here.*

I alerted the others: "Please pray about the tire, it's not looking good." So, we did.

We entered the nuns' area and met one of the Buddhist nuns I knew. She was delighted to see us, made us feel very welcome, and offered us some tea to drink. She then listened with interest as we shared about Jesus, even asking us questions, before we all went for a really enjoyable walk together. After a good two hours, the team were tiring (this type of outreach can be quite exhausting), and we felt it was time to go.

I hadn't said anything about the puncture to the nun but I was very doubtful, wondering whether any of the monks would be available to help us change the wheel. Oh ye of little faith! To my amazement, though, when we got back to the car it was clear that we didn't need to do anything. Although I had actually seen and heard the tire going down, it was fine! We quickly jumped into the car and left, knowing we were "riding on a miracle." We were very happy, rejoicing and thanking God all the way home, aware that something remarkable was happening as we journeyed along!

"Indeed, he who watches over Israel shall neither slumber nor sleep." (Ps 121:4)

For days after, I kept asking people: "Have you ever heard a tire hissing and watched it go down, but it didn't go flat?"

Thank you, Lord!

(For a summary of some of the important differences between Buddhism and Christianity I have mentioned in this book, please see the table in "Exploring Further 14" on page 143.)

We have looked at evangelizing Buddhists. Now let's take a brief look at what kind of discipleship is helpful for Buddhists once they come to Christ.

Chapter 10

Discipleship after Darkness

". . . that you may become blameless and harmless, children of God without fault in the midst of a crooked and perverse generation, among whom you shine as lights in the world, holding fast the word of life." (Phil 2:15–16b nkjv)

"The old verities, the true nature of God and of His revelation to us in and through Christ, can never be compromised, much less surrendered. There are things we can disagree about, and variously stress, but we must always and earnestly contend for the essentials of the faith."[1]

When I left the Buddhist temple, God led me straight to a very sound, Bible-believing church with mature leadership. I am so grateful for that, for with almost no Christian background to speak of I wasn't in much of a position to tell one church from another.

The vicar and his wife, Rev. Will and Rosemary Whitehouse, were so welcoming and wonderfully equipped to mentor and disciple me, despite having only a little knowledge of Buddhism themselves. The teaching and prayer I received in my first three years of being a Christian provided a firm foundation on which to build my Christian life.

---

1. Payne, *Restoring the Christian Soul*, 193.

If you have the choice, though, what kind of church and Christian discipleship would be most helpful for a former Buddhist who has come to know Jesus?

I am thinking here not so much about a denomination—in Thailand we work cross-denominationally, which, I must say, is something I really enjoy—as about the characteristics of a church. Here are some pointers that I suggest will be helpful:

- Look for *mature leadership*, where the church's leader is the type of Christian you aspire to become. A church leader cannot make disciples unless he or she is a disciple themselves. They will not take others beyond what they have let God do in them.

- Seek a church where Christ is central, which has not only *sound teaching* of the Word of God but also church leaders who aspire to *live* by it. Through their loving obedience to Jesus, they keep close to him and so are able to easily follow his leading regarding the church and its members. As it says in Scripture: "By this we know that we love the children of God [our brothers and sisters in the faith], when we love God and keep His commandments" (1 John 5:2 nkjv).

- Such leaders are able to address difficulties and challenges according to biblical standards, which produces an underlying and incredibly valuable sense of security among the church's members. In contrast, those Christian leaders who propose an alternative way to God's Word, however well-meaning their motives, don't seem to see an end to dialogue and debate, or the confusion and division that follow in their wake.

- Find an *encouraging, warm, and safe community*. Having come out of spiritual deception and darkness, this kind of support will help very much to nurture a new believer's faith.

- Seek a *"healing" community* who are able to pray for your wounds and past and present sins and struggles, and can help you to renounce any idolatry (or can help find other Christians who can).

- Look for a *prayerful community* who are able to speak to, listen to, and hear from God.

- Find a community that *looks outward* in order to serve others.

- *If the church is in a Buddhist country*, a former Buddhist will need wise church leaders who know which parts of the nation's culture and traditions Christians are able to participate in; who will help in setting godly boundaries in that respect; and who will support in standing firm when faced with family or other social situations involving Buddhist/idolatrous ceremonies and customs that are no longer appropriate to take part in.

Here are a few examples of the kind of church I suggest you might want to avoid, introduced by a quote of A. W. Tozer with some of his thoughts on the church's decline:

> "The Church has surrendered her once lofty concept of God and has substituted for it one so low, so ignoble, as to be utterly unworthy of thinking, worshiping men. This she has done not deliberately, but little by little and without her knowledge; and her very unawareness only makes her situation all the more tragic."[2]

Does the church embrace "unholy mixtures"? Does it accept such practices as Buddhist meditation, yoga, reiki, and reflexology?

Here are two stories to illustrate this point. Some time back, a friend alerted me to the fact that some high level church leaders of a well-known denomination in the UK had organized a "Buddhist Spirituality Day." The reason they gave was that "we have something to learn from Buddhist methods of meditation, which have a stilling and concentrating effect which Christians can usefully employ in their own prayer."

My "alarm bells" went off, so I wrote to the head of this church explaining I had been a Buddhist nun and of the dangers I saw in mixing Christianity and Buddhism in this way. It was to no avail, though, as he continued to allow it. Sadly, nearly fifteen years later, a syncretistic (and toxic) mixture of Buddhist meditation and Christian prayer is still being taught in this denomination, though thankfully in only a few of its churches.

On another occasion, in America, I met a Christian woman who told me, rather brazenly, that she and her daughter were practicing yoga. She felt it was fine as they were "only doing it for the exercise and nothing else." I immediately cautioned her against it, explaining that it is not possible to separate the physical aspect of yoga from its spiritual roots at a deeper level—they are connected. She didn't heed my warning, however.

2. Tozer, *The Knowledge of the Holy*, vii.

A few months later, she came back to me quite disturbed. Her daughter was under demonic oppression and wanted me to pray for her. I asked if they were now ready to renounce practicing yoga, which they were, so I agreed to see them, and a friend and I prayed for them. Sadly, this family had to learn the hard way.

As we have seen already, we cannot entertain syncretistic spiritual mixtures and remain safe. *The embracing of this kind of idolatry is subtle. If such mixtures are endorsed by church leaders, it shows that they have not fully recognized either idolatry and its dangers or the dark spiritual roots such practices have.*

A better understanding and clearer teaching on this subject is definitely needed, I think, to help our church leaders discern what is appropriate and what is not.

Here is a prayer for those church leaders who humbly wish to acknowledge they have embraced such mixtures:

> *Dear Heavenly Father, I am so sorry that I have allowed such unholy mixtures in your church and have avoided dealing with them. I truly repent and turn from all of them. I will no longer allow [please name it—Buddhist meditation/yoga/reiki/reflexology/etc.] to be tolerated in the church and will endeavor to alert members of the church to their danger. Please forgive me. In Jesus' name I pray. Amen.*

Is the church caught up in a frenzy of meaningless religious activities while avoiding real growth and maturing in Christ?

As Jesus noticed in some of those people around him:

> "Woe to you, scribes and Pharisees, hypocrites! For you are like whitewashed tombs which indeed appear beautiful outwardly, but inside are full of dead men's bones and all uncleanness." (Matt 23:27 nkjv)

What do I mean by that? Such a church is characterized by leaders and members whose schedules are overly full of endless programs, religious activities, and good works.

Please don't misunderstand me, these things are certainly not bad in themselves; but they need to be inspired and led by God if they are to bear real fruit (John 15:5–8). As activity, disconnected from receptivity to God, becomes *activism*—it is then no longer true activity as God intended it to be. It easily becomes all-consuming: restless, driven, exhausting. In fact, some church leaders have been running so fast for so long they have all but forgotten how to stop.

Such a church may appear to be making an impact but at core it can actually be avoiding the teaching and living-out of the truth, which is effectively resisting the purposes of Christ. It has "a form of godliness but denying its power" (2 Tim 3:5), and it is characterized by its lack of power, and remains immature and ineffectual in spite of its endless activities (Jer 12:13a).

Leanne Payne puts it so well:

> "The unaffirmed and unhealed, separated from or refusing the healing administrations and oversight of a mature church and leadership, often seek to find identity, vindication, and meaning in and through their roles or gifts—not in and through Christ. This plight appears over and over again in the church. A deadly activism attempts to fill in and compensate for all else that is lacking and unhealed in a life."[3]

Although clearly found elsewhere in the world, I have noticed a crop of churches like this in Thailand. Paradoxically, I have rarely seen Christians work so hard or such long hours and, equally, have rarely seen Christians take sin so lightly.

What I have described here is actually not so far from what we find in Buddhism: a doctrine not of grace but of "being saved" through *doing*—making merit in order to "pay off" bad actions and avoid a bad rebirth.

Such thinking runs deep in the Thai mind—so much so that this type of church, I would say, is attractive to former Buddhists who are more familiar with doing "good works" than depending on God's grace or dealing with their own very real issues.

Ultimately, the organization and its activities have become its goal, rather than God—and those who accept this substitute will then serve its idolatrous end.

Is it a worldly church, rather than one that experiences and rejoices in the uniqueness and uprightness of Christian living?

I think David F. Wells describes worldliness very well here:

3. Payne, *Heaven's Calling*, 97.

"Worldliness is whatever any culture does to make sin seem normal and righteousness to be strange."[4]

Be careful to avoid a church that gradually loosens the Christian's moral and spiritual framework making it more and more like the world's. In such a church, for instance, sin is no longer named and identified for what it is, but is accommodated, and often given a "nicer, less offensive" label.

When God's holy boundaries between good and evil begin to be blurred in such a way, it serves only to weaken the church's members to fall into such sin themselves. Immorality is often rife as, unaddressed, it is in effect given free rein. To add to the confusion, such a church may not deny the truth of Scripture but actually takes little notice of it in its life and practice.

Christians who live in this way will lose their true relationship with and knowledge of Jesus, along with the purity and beauty of life that he died for us to have.

Or is it a liberal church? I have heard liberal Christians described as "the unbelieving believers." They call themselves Christians but don't completely agree with the Word of God. They are happy to accept the bits they like but, with well-formed arguments, whittle away at those they don't. Their objections, I've noticed, are often grounded in "human compassion," projecting human feelings and values onto a situation rather than biblical ones.

However, as Oswald Chambers says:

"God never fits His word to suit me; He fits me to suit His word."[5]

(Just to say that, even for such churches as mentioned above, there is always hope for change. Effective change, however, will include such things as: the church leadership being willing to give the church back to Jesus once more; confession of sin; and repentance.)

I have already shared much on the subject of Christian discipleship throughout this book. Here then, is a summary of those things I consider to

---

4. From David F. Wells, *God in the Wasteland*, Grand Rapids: Eerdmans, 1995, 59. Quoted in Beale, *We Become What We Worship*, 300.

5. Chambers, *Still Higher for His Highest*, March 11.

be most helpful for people coming out of Buddhism and desiring to grow in Christian maturity, introduced by a quote from Oswald Chambers:

> "Our Lord builds His deepest teaching on the instinct of emulation. When His Spirit comes in He makes me desire not to be inferior to Him Who called me. Our example is not a good man, not even a good Christian man, but God Himself. By the grace of God I have to emulate my Father in heaven. "Be ye therefore perfect, even as your Father which is in heaven is perfect" (Matt. 5:48). The most natural instinct of the supernatural life of God within me is to be worthy of my Father. To say that the doctrine of sanctification is unnatural is not true; the doctrine is based on the way God has made us. When we are born again we become natural for the first time; as long as we are in sin we are abnormal, because sin is not normal."[6]

1. Confession of all past and present sin, including:

   - prayer to renounce Buddhism, idolatry, and/or the occult (see "Exploring Further 4," page 123)
   - prayer to confess relational idolatry and/or sexual immorality (see "Exploring Further 7," page 129, and possibly also the prayer for renouncing Baal and Ashtoreth in "Exploring Further 9" on page 133 if applicable)
   - prayer to break generational ties (see "Exploring Further 12," page 139)

2. Prayers for empowering and strengthening, including:

   - prayer for inner healing for our past wounds and brokenness (this is not included at the back of this book, but please ask your church leaders for help with this, or guidance to know where to go)
   - prayer for a "sense of being" (see "Exploring Further 1," page 119)
   - prayer for the "empowering of our wills" (see "Exploring Further 3," page 122)

3. The daily putting-on of the full armor of God (Eph 6:11–18)

---

6. Chambers, op. cit., March 2.

4. The renewing of our minds

   Former Buddhists need their minds renewed and redeemed. The following things I found to be a great help: regular attendance at church, joining a cell or home group as recommended by the church leaders, and daily "quiet times" in order to read the Bible, pray, and worship God by yourself. In fact, all the good Christian disciplines will help to renew and strengthen our minds.

5. A prayer and accountability partner

   It is very helpful to have a (same gender) prayer and accountability partner: someone safe and mature with whom we can meet every two-to-four weeks to pray for each other and confess sin together. I have found this extremely beneficial as a regular part of my Christian life. And, even though I travel a lot, when I find myself in a new situation, I pray for a prayer partner and it's usually not long before the Lord provides one!

6. Dwelling on Christian symbols

   As someone who focused on Buddha and idols for so many years, I love to dwell on Christian symbols now such as the cross and the Communion bread and cup. This is not to make idols of these symbols but to let the Christian reality and truth they represent seep in and nourish our souls.

7. Choosing to live in obedience to God's Word

   A great stabilizing and enabling factor in Christian growth, is the degree to which we say and believe that the Word of God is our standard of righteousness, and the level to which we allow Jesus to help us live this out in every area of daily life. If that seems to be a distant possibility, begin to pray to God, alone or with others, for help to realize it.

   "Finally, brothers and sisters, whatever is true, whatever is noble, whatever is right [*just*, nkjv], whatever is pure, whatever is lovely, whatever is admirable—if anything is excellent or praiseworthy—think about such things." (Phil 4:8)

Conclusion

Having started with the quest for truth, and endeavored through two books now to share with you the essence of that journey, I am so glad that you have been able to join in some of it with me, too!

As we have seen, things are not always what they appear and it is incredibly easy to be deceived, even when we are truly sincere in our search. We look for signs that will help to direct us and some of the most convincing only serve to send us down a rocky path and deep into a "ravine" before we realize how lost we are.

In this book, I have sought to explain some important differences between Buddhism and Christianity as well as to reveal the nature of Buddhism as I now see it "from the other side." *People who are coming out of Buddhism to faith in Jesus Christ have to leave not only Buddhism but an idolatrous mindset. This is not easy, and One much greater than both of these is needed.*

Mercifully for us, Jesus waits patiently until we can recognize our need of him—until finally we "ask and it will be given to [us]; seek and [we] will find; knock and the door will be opened to [us]" (Matt 7:7).

However long and hard our journey, this quest for truth is completely and utterly worth pursuing, with unimaginable heights awaiting those who humbly persist. As Leanne Payne says:

> "Truth is so beautiful and without limit, and our walk is in the presence of Truth Himself. He directs, guides, teaches, reproves, and never stops speaking wisdom and knowledge into the darkened spaces of our minds and hearts. And always, even when we are the weakest, He gives strength for the journey—not only for

the terrible spiritual battles but for the great victories as well. His path is a blessed one; it is fruitful and it is holy."[1]

Thinking about how deeply committed to Buddhism I once was and how lost I have been at times, and what great love and mercy Jesus has shown to me, I can't help but think that if he can help me, there is great hope for any Buddhist (or idolater), however strong their commitment to it may be.

As it says in Rev 22:17b:

> "Let the one who is thirsty come; and let the one who wishes take the free gift of the water of life."

1. Payne, *Heaven's Calling*, 159–160.

Exploring Further 1
Prayer for a Sense of Being

Those coming out of Buddhism often lack a sense of being, which of course, is not helped by the Buddhist goal of non-being. If you have experienced strong feelings of anxiety, abandonment, emptiness, and loneliness, it would be good to receive prayer that *the dreadful sense of non-being be replaced with a solid sense of being, a true self within,* where you can receive and contain God's love and affirmation.

It would be helpful to have a mature Christian pray this through with you:

Heavenly Father,

Like David, who likened himself to a "weaned child with his mother" [Psalm 131:2], I enter into your presence. I acknowledge you, Father, to be the steadfast and tender One. I come to you seeking your affirmation and confirmation. With the help of the Holy Spirit, I avail to you the deep-seated emptiness, fear and anxiety that have pervaded my life. Envelop me with your loving, steadfast presence. By your grace, secure in me the very ground of my being that my mother and/or those who nurtured me were somehow unable to confirm in me. Free me to receive your love, as the Creator and Redeemer of my life. Become the ground of my security as a person. Free me to live out of your loving initiative toward me. In Jesus' name I pray. Amen.[1]

"Truly God alone can speak *being* into a soul that failed to come to an adequate sense of being."[2]

---

1. Based on a prayer written by Comiskey, *Living Waters*, 26, and similar to the prayer in *I Once was a Buddhist Nun*, 147.
2. Payne, *Heaven's Calling*, 297.

Exploring Further 2
The Simple Gospel Message—an Outline

Jesus is the Son of God, sent to earth to die on the cross for our sins. All the sin—past, present, and future—of fallen humanity was taken upon Jesus on the cross. He died and on the third day he rose again. He overcame the power of sin, death, and hell, and is now seated at the right hand of God the Father.

If we acknowledge to God that we have sinned, and we invite Jesus to be Lord of our lives, our sins are forgiven; we enter into a personal relationship with him, we become children of God, and we inherit eternal life as we walk in obedience to him (Heb 12:14b; Rev 21:8).

Salvation means coming into relationship with the Father through Jesus. It is a free gift, and we can do nothing to earn it—we just have to accept it freely.

> "For God so loved the world that he gave his one and only Son,
> that whoever believes in him shall not perish but have eternal life."
> (John 3:16)

PRAYER TO INVITE JESUS INTO YOUR LIFE:

Here is a simple prayer that anyone can pray who does not yet know Jesus and would like to invite him into their life. I would encourage anyone who prays this prayer to get in touch with a local Bible-believing Christian church that can help and support them in their walk with God.

Dear Lord Jesus,

I know that I am a sinner. I am sorry for all that I have done wrong and ask you to forgive me. Thank you for dying on the cross for me. I invite you now to come into my life. I receive you as my Savior, Lord, and Master. I place my whole life into your hands. Thank you for your cleansing and forgiveness, and the gift of eternal life.

In your name I pray. Amen.

Exploring Further 3
Prayer for the Empowering of Your Will

Father God, I confess that living under deception has brought about a crippling lethargy and passivity. My will has become weak. I have great need of your strength to empower and restore me.

I thank you that I can trust you. I pray that you come by your Holy Spirit and empower my will that has become weakened, even atrophied.

Help me, Father, to receive your strength and enlivening, so that I can rise up anew with a will empowered to stand against darkness and deception. I choose to rise up out of weakness as I look to you, Lord Jesus. Help me to walk and live according to your holy will, in that place of grace and truth where my will is aligned with yours.

In Jesus' name I pray. Amen.

Exploring Further 4
Prayer for Renouncing Buddhism, Idolatry, and/or the Occult[1]

The prayer below can be used to renounce any (past or present) involvement with Buddhism, idolatry, and/or the occult and may be adapted according to your needs. Ideally, it should be prayed under the leadership of one or two mature Christians, who can also offer a prayer of cleansing and blessing afterwards.

If there are many things to renounce, it is helpful to take time before the prayer session to prepare a list—it is important to do a thorough job in order to make a clean cut from these things. Each idol and/or occult activity should be named, renounced, and repented of in Jesus' name.

Additionally, any Buddha statues, images of idols, amulets, charms, books, etc., need to be destroyed, ideally before this prayer is said. God needs to see commitment in action as well as words, which is the meaning of true repentance.

> *Dear Lord Jesus,*
>
> *I come to you now and enter into your presence. Before you, I repent of the sin of having being involved in [Buddhism/idolatry/the occult]. I renounce it and turn away from it. [I also renounce Buddhist ways of thinking that have kept me bound.] I ask Lord Jesus, that you cut and destroy the relationship I have had with [Buddhism/idolatry/the occult] so that it no longer has any power or influence over my life. Please forgive me for my idolatry. Please wash me clean me from the effects of it by your blood. Help me to see idolatry and detest it as you do.*

1. Based on the prayer from *I Once was a Buddhist Nun,* 147–148.

> *I pray Lord Jesus that you renew my mind. Help me to focus on you, to have my needs met in you, and to grow into the fullness of life that you intend me for to have. Thank you, Lord Jesus. In your name I pray. Amen.*

The person praying with the one renouncing Buddhism, idolatry, and/or the occult might use words like these:

> *Thank You, Lord Jesus, for [name]'s prayer. Thank you that you now stand between [name] and [Buddhism/idolatry/the occult]. Please break any relationship and connection that [name] has had with [Buddhism/idolatry/the occult] so that [he/she] is totally free from it. Please wash and cleanse [name]'s mind—even [his/her] subconscious mind—and body, soul, and spirit completely from the effects of [Buddhism/idolatry/the occult].*

> *Thank you that you died to set [name] free, and for your promise: "I will sprinkle clean water on you, and you will be clean; I will cleanse you from all your impurities and from all your idols."[2]*

> *Please fill [name] with your Holy Spirit. Help [him/her] to guard [his/her] mind; renew [his/her] mind and give [him/her] "the mind of Christ."[3] Bless [name]'s true self as you have made [him/her] to be. Thank you for the new freedom [name] now has in you. In your name I pray. Amen.*

2. Ezek 36:25.

3. 1 Cor 2:16.

Exploring Further 5
Names of Jesus and His Enemy

Throughout this book, we have come across some descriptive names of both Jesus and his enemy. This (by no means comprehensive) list draws some of them together for you, including, both some found in the text, as well as those that are not.

NAMES OF JESUS

the *Almighty* (Rev 1:8)
the *author and finisher of our faith* (Heb 12:2 nkjv)
the *Beginning and the End* (Rev 22:13)
the *bread of life* (John 6:35)
the *bridegroom* (Matt 25:10)
the *bright Morning Star* (Rev 22:16)
the *deliverer* (Rom 11:26)
the *door* (John 10:9 nkjv)
the *eternal life* (1 John 1:2; 5:20)
the *Faithful and True* (Rev 19:11)
the *good shepherd* (John 10:11, 14)
the *head of the church* (Eph 1:22; 4:15; 5:23)
the *hope of glory* (Col 1:27)
Immanuel (Matt 1:23)
the *judge of the living and the dead* (Acts 10:42)
the *Just One* (Acts 7:52 nkjv)
KING OF KINGS AND LORD OF LORDS (Rev 19:16)
the *King of the nations* (Rev 15:3)
the *Lamb of God* (John 1:29)

the *life* (John 14:6)

the *light of the world* (John 8:12)

the *mediator between God and humankind* (1 Tim 2:5 nrsv)

the *Prince of Peace* (Isa 9:6)

the *resurrection and the life* (John 11:25)

the *Righteous One* (Acts 7:52; 1 John 2:1)

the *Savior of the world* (1 John 4:14)

the *Son of God* (John 1:49; Heb 4:14)

the *Son of Man* (Matt 8:20; Mark 10:33)

the *true God* (1 John 5:20)

the *truth* (John 14:6)

the *vine* (John 15:5)

the *way* (John 14:6)

the *wisdom of God* (1 Cor 1:24)

the *Word* (John 1:1)

NAMES OF JESUS' ENEMY

Satan (Rev 12:9), a Hebrew word meaning "the adversary"

the *accuser* (Rev 12:10)

the *ancient snake* (Rev 12:9)

the *devil* (1 John 3:8; Rev 12:9)

the *dragon* (Rev 20:2)

the *evil one* (John 17:15)

the *god of this age* (2 Cor 4:4)

the *prince or ruler* (nkjv) *of this world* (John 14:30)

the *prince of the power of the air* (nkjv) or the *ruler of the kingdom of the air* (Eph 2:2)

the *tempter* (Matt 4:3)

the *wicked one* (1 John 5:18–19 nkjv)

Exploring Further 6
Different Types of Idolatry

Here are a few examples of what can become idols for us.

IDOLATRY OF SELF

Self-centered idolatry: physical beauty/physique, intelligence, education, career, fame, achievements, money, investments, property, possessions

The pursuit of pleasure: food, clothes, sport, hobbies, travel, computer games, TV, films and DVD, radio, romantic novels

IDOLATRY OF OTHERS

Relational idolatry: emotional dependency on another person (opposite sex or same sex), boyfriend, girlfriend, husband, wife, family members, friends, pop or film stars, leaders, teachers, care-givers, former or present kings, queens, presidents, and historical figures

People in the church: gifted individuals, those who have helped us, those who need us

Sexual idolatry: sexual addictions of various kinds, internet pornography, adultery, use of prostitutes, incest, fantasy life

SPIRITUAL IDOLATRY

New Age, druidism, human philosophies, ideologies, idols made with human hands, ancient gods such as Baal and Ashtoreth, heavenly bodies (sun, moon, stars), anything in nature that is considered sacred (trees, animals, mountains), witchcraft and the occult, use of mediums, superstition, palmistry, tarot cards, past lives, ancestor worship, rocks, and crystals

In the church: idolatrous relationship to Christian ministry and/or service, idolatrous attachment to style of Christian liturgy and worship, tradition, legalism

Exploring Further 7

Prayer for the Confession of Relational Idolatry and/or Sexual Immorality

The prayer below can be used when confessing past or present relational idolatry (emotional dependency) and/or sexual immorality. Ideally, it should be prayed under the leadership of a safe and mature Christian who can also offer a prayer of cleansing and blessing afterwards.

(It will be a great help toward the freedom of the person praying this, if he/she is able to destroy or give up any photographs of or gifts from those they have been in bondage to, before this prayer is said.)

> *Dear Lord Jesus,*
>
> *I thank you that you are here with us. Before you now, I confess my sin(s) of relational idolatry and/or sexual immorality [please be specific and name it: relational idolatry with someone of the opposite sex and/or the same sex; addiction to pornography; fantasy life; and so on].*
>
> *I give my sin(s) to you, and choose to turn away from it. As I seek your healing forgiveness, I pray that you will wash me with your blood and cleanse me from this sin and its effects. Help me, dear Lord, to set your holy boundaries in this my area of weakness. Help me to choose to abide increasingly in you, where I find healing and strength. Amen.*

The person praying with the one confessing might use words like these:
Thank you, Lord Jesus, for [name]'s prayer and confession. Please wash [name]'s mind, body, soul, and spirit with your blood, and cleanse him/her completely from the effects of his/her [relational idolatry and/or sexual immorality].

Please clothe [name] in your robe of righteousness and fill him/her afresh with your Holy Spirit. Help [name] to guard his/her heart and mind and to establish your holy boundaries around him/her. Amen.

Exploring Further 8
Romans 1: Explaining the Effects of Idolatry

How does idolatry play such a crucial part in the breakdown of morality, both sexual and otherwise? I find Romans 1, written by the apostle Paul, to be one the Bible's clearest explanations of this. I have italicized key sections of the passage below for emphasis.

Romans 1:20–32:

> 20For since the creation of the world God's invisible qualities—his eternal power and divine nature—have been clearly seen, being understood from what has been made, so that people are without excuse.
>
> 21For although they knew God, they neither glorified him as God nor gave thanks to him, but their thinking became futile and their foolish hearts were darkened. 22Although they claimed to be wise, they became fools 23and *exchanged the glory of the immortal God for images [idols]* made to look like a mortal human being and birds and animals and reptiles.
>
> 24Therefore *God gave them over in the sinful desires of their hearts* to sexual impurity for the degrading of their bodies with one another. 25They exchanged the truth about God for a lie, and worshipped and served created things rather than the Creator—who is for ever praised. Amen.
>
> 26Because of this, *God gave them over to shameful lusts*. Even their women exchanged natural sexual relations for unnatural ones. 27In the same way the men also abandoned natural relations with women and were inflamed with lust for one another. Men committed shameful acts with other men, and received in themselves the due penalty for their error.
>
> 28Furthermore, just as they did not think it worth while to retain the knowledge of God, so *God gave them over to a depraved*

mind, so that they do what ought not to be done. 29They have become filled with every kind of wickedness, evil, greed and depravity. They are full of envy, murder, strife, deceit and malice. They are gossips, 30slanderers, God-haters, insolent, arrogant and boastful; they invent ways of doing evil; they disobey their parents; 31they have no understanding, no fidelity, no love, no mercy. 32Although they know God's righteous decree that those who do such things deserve death, they not only continue to do these very things but also approve of those who practise them.

Let's take a closer look at this passage.

Paul writes that God has made himself known to us through creation (v. 20)—it's as if he has signed his artwork for us all to see. But the thoughts of those who do not glorify God nor are thankful to him become futile— empty and confused—and their hearts are darkened (v. 21). They think they are wise but they are actually fools (v. 22).

Even though they are in rebellion to God and impious towards him, they still carry an inborn desire and need to worship. Their gaze falls upon and their devotion is given to something created (v. 23)—*idols*—substitutes for the living God. In doing this, they elevate that part of creation above its rightful place—over its Creator. Their devotion to idols serves to keep them away from God and continues to distort their understanding of him and of his creation, having "exchanged the truth about God for a lie" (v. 25).

Such idolatrous worship has very significant consequences. It's as if God's "protective hand" is removed from them and God gives them over (a phrase repeated three times, in vv. 24, 26, and 28) to:

- sinful desires

- shameful lusts—turning from natural human relations to unnatural ones

- a debased mind

In other words, *rebellion against God through idolatry leads to God giving people up to increasing immorality and perversion, both sexual (vv. 26–27) and otherwise.* They become enslaved by their idolatry and sin and suffer the consequences of it. Their humanity is distorted and corrupted: "filled with every kind of evil and depravity" (vv. 29–31), which was never God's intention for them. *That which never was, nor did God intend to be, nor can he ever bless, comes into existence. What was once unthinkable can now become attractive and even treated as the "norm." And not only are they caught up in it but they approve of others who do the same (v. 32).*

Exploring Further 9
Prayer to Renounce Baal and Ashtoreth

This type of idolatrous worship is not confined to such obviously dark places as mentioned in Ying's story—it can even come into the church.

As Andy Comiskey writes:

> "Whenever anyone, Christian or not, yields his [or her] body to another for erotic gratification outside the heterosexual covenant [that is, God's marriage covenant], he makes a sacrifice to Baal. The principality of sexual perversion is alive and well. We bow down to it whenever we engage in sexual immorality."[1]

The "worship of Baal" has serious and disturbing effects. I have met and ministered to Christians, both men and women, Western and Asian, who have been bombarded with phallic images and are unable to get them out of their minds. The solution is to clearly acknowledge your sin and repent, truly turning away from all forms of sexual immorality and perversion, and to renounce the idol gods of Baal (representing more the male aspect of sexuality) and/or Ashtoreth (representing more the female aspect of sexuality) in Jesus' name. I would recommend that for anyone to whom this is applicable, reading chapter 14 of Leanne Payne's book *The Healing Presence* would be most helpful. It is important to note that some people who are deeply wounded will need careful inner healing prayer *before* they are ready to pray this prayer of renunciation.

> "Put to death, therefore, whatever belongs to your earthly nature: sexual immorality, impurity, lust, evil desires and greed, which is idolatry." (Col 3:5)

---

1. Comiskey, *Pursuing Sexual Wholeness*, 100.

I would encourage you to pray this in the presence of a safe and mature Christian, who understands the need for such a prayer and who can pray a prayer of cleansing and blessing over you afterwards:

> *I confess, Lord Jesus, that I have set up idols in my heart, which I now repent of. I confess that I have bent the knee to gods of sexual idolatry, immorality, and/or perversion. In the name of Jesus, I choose to renounce all false idol gods, especially Baal and/or Ashtoreth. I renounce you, Baal. I renounce you, Ashtoreth. I pray, Lord Jesus, that you would free me from them and wash and cleanse me with your blood from the effects of worshiping them. In your name, I pray. Amen.*

The person praying with the one renouncing Baal and/or Ashtoreth might use words like these:

> *Dear Lord Jesus, please wash [name] with your blood deep in his/her mind, body, soul, and spirit, so that he/she is cleansed from the effects of worshiping Baal and/or Ashtoreth.*

> *Lord Jesus, please sever him/her from these gods of sexual idolatry so that he/she will be free to worship you in spirit and in truth. Help [name] to turn away from old ways of thinking and being and to fix his/her gaze on you. Bless and strengthen him/her in all goodness and righteousness. Please fill him/her afresh with your Holy Spirit, I pray. In Jesus' name I pray. Amen.*

Exploring Further 10

Nature of Idols/Idolatry and God

Nature of Idols/Idolatry	Nature of God
idols are **not God** (Deut 32:21)	God is the **true God** (Jer 10:10; 1 John 5:20)
idols are **not above God** (Deut 10:17)	God is **above all gods** (Deut 10:17; Zeph 2:11)
idols are lifeless, **dead** (Pss 115:5–7)	God is **alive for evermore** (Jer 10:10, Rev 1:18)
idols are often the **work of human hands** (2 Kgs 19:18; Ps 115:4) and have to be carried around (Isa 46:1, 7)	God is **not made with hands**—he is unformed, uncreated (Gen 1:1a; 1 Tim 1:17). He is everywhere and does not have to be carried around (Pss 139:7–12)
idols **cannot compare to the true God** (Isa 46:5, 9; 1 Kgs 18:21–40) and have no agreement with God (2 Cor 6:16a)	God **cannot be compared to idols** (Isa 46:5, 9; 1 Kgs 18:21–40) and has no agreement with them (2 Cor 6:16a)
idols are nothing, **know nothing**, are **worthless** (Isa 41:23–24; 44:9–18)	God **is all-knowing** (Pss 139:1–6) and we **cannot measure his worth** (Rev 5:12)
idols **cannot speak, see, hear, smell, touch or walk** (Pss 115:5–7)	God **loves to communicate** with his people (Exod 3); the Word (Jesus) **became flesh and walked among us** (John 1:14)
idolatry **leads to moral decay, spiritual corruption, and lawlessness** (Exod 32:6; Rom 1:18–32)	God **is the source of all virtue and goodness** (Deut 32:4, Ps 33:5; 89:14), **pure and without sin** (2 Cor 5:21), and desires that we are holy, too (Deut 7:6; 1 Pet 1:16)
idolatry, the occult, and immorality are often **found together** (Exod 32:6; Rev 9:20–21)	God **forbids his people** to practice **idolatry, the occult, and immorality** (Deut 18:9–14)

idols **harm us** (Jer 7:6, Ps 81:12) and bring shame (Isa 45:16; Jer 8:1–2; 13:25–27), vulnerability and chaos (Rom 1:24, 26, 28)	God **desires to bless and honor us** (Deut 28:1–14) and protect us (2 Tim 4:18)
idols **teach lies** (Hab 2:18), are **frauds** (Jer 10:14) and cause truth to vanish (Jer 7:28b)	God **is truth** (John 14:6) and is **covenant-al and faithful** (Gen 6:18)
idolatry **starves our imaginations** and increasingly **takes over our minds** (Jer 2:20–25; 13:27). It easily leads to darker spiritual practices and **greater bondage** (Jer 7:31)	God **blesses our imaginations** (Isa 40:26) and **gives us a sound mind** (2 Tim 1:7), the mind of Christ (1 Cor 2:16), and **true freedom** (John 8:36)
idolatry is **sacrifice to demons** (Deut 32:17 nkjv; 1 Cor 10:20–21)	God **sees idolatry as evil** (Deut 4:25) and abhors it (Ps 78:58), and wants idols destroyed (Deut 7:1–6, 25–26; 9:21)
idolatry **leads us to emptiness** (Jer 2:5 nasb)	God **leads us to fullness of life** (John 10:10)

Exploring Further 11

Some Important Differences between Idolaters and God's Intent for Christians

Idolaters:	(God intends that) Christians:
worship many idols/gods, sometimes mixed in with impure worship of God (2 Kgs 17:33; 23:1–25), are often "open and eclectic," **find themselves in the created**, not the Creator (Rom 1:25), and **set their minds on earthly things**, and exalt the created above its natural importance (Jer 10:11; Rom 1:23)	**worship God alone** (Deut 6:4; 2 Kgs 17:36); **worship the Creator, not what is created** (Gen 1:1; Isa 40:21–22); find themselves in God (Mal 3:17–18; 1 Cor 1:30); honor God in his rightful place—high and lifted up (Gen 14:18; Ps 47:2); and **set their minds on things above** (Phil 4:8)
love idols (Isa 57:5–9) and are "God-haters" (Rom 1:30). They are **characterized by unfaithfulness** and commit "spiritual adultery" (Hos 13:2), having many gods and, often, many sexual partners, too	**stay far from idols** (Deut 12:1–4; 2 Cor 6:16–7:1). Are **characterized by faithfulness**—one God and one husband or wife of the opposite sex (Jer 3:1). God calls us to love him purely and wholeheartedly, as "a wife to a husband" (Hos 2:14–23; Eph 5:25b–28), and to be faithful to our spouse (Mal 2:13–16; Matt 5:27)
usually **reject the finality of God's moral authority**, building a philosophy or ideology (such as communism) to justify their idolatry (Rom 1:18–32)	**accept and live by God's moral authority** expressed through his Word (Ps 119; Prov 30:5)
reflect their idols, becoming like the things they love (Ps 115:8; Hos 9:10)	**reflect and become like God** (Rom 8:29; 2 Cor 3:18), participating in the divine nature (2 Pet 1:4)

like their images/idols; they **cannot see, hear, or understand** (Deut 29:2–4; Rom 1:21); they are given over to stubbornness (Pss 81:8–12) and a deluded heart (Isa 44:20)	are **able to see, hear, and understand** (Isa 42:6–7; Rev 3:18) and have the wisdom of God (1 Cor 1:30; Col 2:2b–3)
exchange the glory of God for what does not profit (Jer 2:11 nkjv)—**the image of corruption**: a human being, birds, animals (Rom 1:23 nkjv) and of a bull that eats grass (Ps 106:20)	**behold the glory of the Lord and be transformed into his image** (2 Cor 3:18). Jesus will transform our lowly bodies to be like his glorious body (Phil 3:21)
forfeit God's love and mercy, which could be theirs (Jonah 2:8)	**receive God's love and mercy** (Rom 5:2)
approve of others who are **idolaters and evildoers** (Rom 1:32)	**flee from idolatry** (1 Cor 10:14) and reject every kind of evil (1 Thess 5:22), considering themselves dead to sin but alive to God in Jesus Christ (Rom 6:11)
will not enter the kingdom of heaven (1 Cor 6:9–10; Gal 5:19–21) but will end in the lake that burns with fire, or hell (Rev 21:8; 22:15)	**will enter the kingdom of heaven** into God's presence and have eternal life—ever more becoming through his Son Jesus (John 17:3; 1 John 5:11b–12; Rev 21:1–7)

Exploring Further 12
Prayer for Breaking Generational Ties

"If they will confess their sins and the sins of their ancestors–their unfaithfulness and their hostility towards me—I will remember my covenant." (Lev 26:40, 42, see also Deut 5:7, 9)

The following (basic) prayer can be used for breaking generational ties. Ideally it should be prayed under the leadership of a mature Christian.

To start with, together, you may like to invite the Lord Jesus to lead this prayer time. Also to ask him for any "words of knowledge" (1 Cor 12:7–11) he may wish to give you concerning specific areas of sin or bondage that have come down to you from past generations, which you may have forgotten about or may not even have been aware of.

Before receiving prayer, you can share about any known areas of sin or bondage in your family line which have come into your own life; for instance, your mother was a Buddhist and your grandmother was a medium.

Dear Lord Jesus,

I thank you for the blessings that have come down to me through my family line. But now, I come to you seeking to be free of any sin, idolatry, and bondage that have come to me, inherited from former generations. Thank you, Lord Jesus, that you died for me to set me free and that your blood has power over sin, generational and otherwise. I ask you now to set me free and rid me of any bondage of my ancestors that still has power over my life.

[Beginning with the fifth generation back and continuing down to the fourth, third, etc.], I confess and renounce the sins of this generation of my ancestors. [If known, please name the person(s) and

139

sin(s) specifically; if not known, this general prayer will suffice.] I ask you, Lord, to take the sword of the Spirit and break any stronghold, whether spiritual or psychological or of any other kind. Please wash me clean in that very place of former bondage and defilement with your blood, and fill me afresh with your Holy Spirit. Thank you that you are my protector and defense as I walk in obedience to you. I pray this in your name. Amen.

Exploring Further 13
Summary of Preparations and Procedure in Evangelizing Buddhists

- Prepare yourself. Are you right with God? Is there any sin or idolatry you need to confess and renounce? Put on "the full armor of God" (Eph 6:11–17).

- Wherever possible, don't go alone (Mark 6:6). Pray for one or more people to go with you.

- With your team/friend, pray for God's timing (Exod 33:15), strategy, and specific words, pictures, and scriptures for the visit. Sketch out what your team can expect and how they can support one another when with Buddhists.

- Have some friends praying at home or elsewhere while you go, and let them know how you got on after you return.

- Don't be afraid (Josh 1:9). Jesus is with you. It is the Lord's battle and he will protect you and fight for you.

- Stay focused, fixing your eyes on Jesus. Avoid becoming distracted. Be silently praying for one another as you speak to Buddhists. Talk in a non-threatening, matter-of-fact way, avoiding arguments and debates.

- Speak about Jesus as God gives you opportunity, sharing the simple gospel message where possible. Offer to pray for Buddhists and share Scripture with them as the situation allows.

- Don't take an adverse reaction personally—it is not you they are offended by but the cross of Christ.

- Soon after your visit ends, ask the Lord Jesus to cleanse your minds, bodies, souls, and spirits. Check that everyone on your team is feeling okay.

- If possible, have a time of feedback and prayer after your visit. Thank God for what he has done and for his faithfulness. Whether you see results or not, the time has not been wasted.

- Keep praying for the people you have witnessed to.

Exploring Further 14
Some Important Differences between Buddhism and Christianity

Buddhism teaches that:	Christianity teaches that:
because life consists of endless rounds of sorrow and suffering, **the origin of the universe is ignorance** (*avijjā*). "There is no first cause possible as . . . everything is relative and inter-dependent"[1]	**in the beginning God created the heavens and earth** (Gen 1:1) and "saw all that he had made, and it was very good" (Gen 1:31)
Buddha was a human being; he taught that the position of human beings is "supreme" and that each is their own master. His insights came from his own human effort, intelligence, and understanding	**in Jesus all the fullness of God lives in bodily form** (Col 1:19; 2:9). Jesus is supreme (Col 1:15). His insights and understanding are of God
Buddha points the way	**Jesus is the way**
we are not **to rely on** anyone but **ourselves**	**Jesus has done it** all **for us**; our part is to obey him and his Word
the essential problem we have **is ignorance** of the impermanence, unsatisfactoriness, and "selflessness" of all phenomena, **which leads to suffering through endless rebirths**	**the essential problem** we have **is not knowing God** and living according to his ways, **which leads to suffering throughout eternity**
we have no soul, self, or spirit—belief in them comes from delusion	**we have a soul, self, and spirit** (John 1:12; 1 Thess 5:23); our true self is God's crowning glory as we are made in his image

1. Rahula, *What the Buddha Taught*, 29.

"there is no 'sin' in Buddhism, as sin is understood in some religions. The root of all evil is ignorance (*avijjā*) and false views (*micchā diṭṭhi*)"[2]	God clearly defines sin for us (i.e., the Ten Commandments in Exodus 20). We sin when we do not walk in Gods ways, it offends him and it needs to be dealt with (1 Pet 1:16)
karma (and the need to "make merit") and endless births in various realms (the continuing cycle of *saṃsāra*) persist until the realization of nirvāṇa	salvation comes through Jesus' death and resurrection—God's grace, freely given to us. We have one life only (Heb 9:27) and then God determines whether we go to heaven or hell (2 Thess 1:8–9)
the most important thing is to escape suffering	the most important thing is the restoration of our relationship with God the Father through Jesus
practicing meditation and letting go/detachment is necessary in order to escape suffering	Jesus came so that we might have life in all its fullness (John 10:10) and might embrace life—but not sin or evil
prayer to Buddha is not possible, as his aim was to be "fully extinct," and there is no God to pray to	we pray to God
Buddhists have a spiritual goal of eternal extinction, an end of being, no more becoming, in order to escape the cycle of rebirths and therefore suffering.	Christians have a spiritual goal of everlasting life with God (John 3:16–18, 11:25–26), following the resurrection of all believers (John 14:1–5). "He is not the God of the dead but of the living" (Matt 22:32b)

2. Rahula, *What the Buddha Taught*, 3.

Exploring Further 15

Some Important Differences between Nirvāṇa and Eternal Life with God

Nirvāṇa	Eternal Life with God
Buddha who claimed to have realized nirvāṇa, after death, is described as **"fully blown out"** or **"fully extinct"**[1]	**Jesus rose from the dead** (1 Cor 15:4) and ascended into heaven. **He is the power of indestructible life** (Heb 7:16) **and is alive forever** (John 17:3)
the one having realized nirvāṇa, after death, has **nowhere to go**. Referring to nirvāṇa, Buddha said: "there is the un-born, ungrown, and unconditioned"[2]	Jesus said: "I go and prepare a place for you [and] **I will** come again and **receive you to Myself; that where I am, there you may be also**" (John 14:3 nkjv)
there is **no more death or suffering** as the goal is that no one or nothing is born, so no one or nothing can suffer and die	there is **no more death or suffering** as we go beyond death into eternal life in the presence of a holy, loving God. "He will wipe every tear from their eyes. There will be no more death or mourning or crying or pain, for the old order of things has passed away" (Rev 21:4)
nirvāṇa is described as **no more being** and **no more becoming**	we have **everlasting life, eternal being** (John 3:16; 11:25–26; 1 John 5:11b–12), **ever more becoming**
the one having realized nirvāṇa, after death, has **nothing to do and no one or nothing to reflect** as no one or nothing is born	**worshipers of God reflect him and his glory.** Along with other believers, we **will praise God and enjoy him forever** (2 Cor 3:18; Jude 24–25; Rev 21:23)

1. Rahula, *What the Buddha Taught*, 41.
2. Ibid., 37.

a Buddhist is not able to have a relationship with Buddha here on earth, as he is said to be **"fully passed away."**[3] The one having realized nirvāṇa, after death, has **no relationship with anyone or anything** as the goal is that no one or nothing is born	we are **born to have a** godly **relationship and unity with a holy, loving God here on earth and forever, through eternity** (Rev 21:3, 7) **as well as with other believers through eternity** (Rev 5:9b)

3. Rahula, *What the Buddha Taught*, 41.

Helpful Websites

www.alpha.org For those who would like to find out more about Jesus

www.leannepayne.org For helpful books and courses in deepening our relationship with Jesus

www.myutmost.org Helpful books for daily devotion and maturing in our Christian lives

www.ivpbooks.com For information on the author's first book *I Once was a Buddhist Nun*

www.thinkivp.com *I Once . . .* as an e-book

www.fronda.pl *I Once . . .* in Polish: *Bylam buddyjską mniszką*

www.brunnen-verlag.ch *I Once . . .* in German: *Ich war eine buddhistische Nonne*

www.arkmedia.nl *I Once . . .* in Dutch: *Mijn weg van Boeddha naar Christus*

www.paiva.fi *I Once . . .* in Finnish: *Olin buddhalainen nunna*

www.estherbaker.com For further information including the author's contact details

Bibliography

Baker, Esther. *I Once Was a Buddhist Nun*. Nottingham, England: InterVarsity Press, 2009.

Beale, G. K. *We Become What We Worship: A Biblical Theology of Idolatry*. Downers Grove, IL: IVP Academic, 2008.

Burnside, Jonathan. "Covert Power: Unmasking the World of Witchcraft." *Cambridge Papers: Towards a Biblical Mind*. vol. 19, no. 4, December 2010.

Chambers, Oswald. *My Utmost for His Highest*. Classic Edition. Uhrichsville, OH: Barbour Publishing, 1963.

———. *Still Higher for His Highest*. Grand Rapids, MI: Zondervan Publishing House, 1970.

Comiskey, Andrew. *Living Waters: Pursuing Sexual and Relational Wholeness in Christ*. Grandview, MO: Desert Stream Ministries, 1996.

———. *Pursuing Sexual Wholeness: How Jesus Heals the Homosexual*. Lake Mary, FL: Creation House, 1989.

De Neui, Paul H., Editor. *Suffering: Christian Reflections on Buddhist Dukkha*, No.8 in the SEANET Series. Pasadena, CA: William Carey Library, 2011.

Kamphuis, Martin. Unpublished translation of: *Ich war Buddhist*. Bassel: Brunnen Verlag, 2000, used with permission.

O'Brien, Michael. "Harry Potter and the Paganization of Children's Culture." In *Catholic World Report Magazine*, April 21, 2003. Online: http:// www.leannepayne.org/Harry Potter/.

Payne, Leanne. *Heaven's Calling: A Memoir of One Soul's Steep Ascent*. Grand Rapids, MI: Baker Books, 2008.

———. *Listening Prayer: Learning to Hear God's Voice and Keep a Prayer Journal*. Grand Rapids, MI: Hamewith Books, 1994.

———. *Real Presence: The Glory of Christ With Us and Within Us*. Grand Rapids, MI: Hamewith Books, 1995.

———. *Restoring the Christian Soul: Overcoming Barriers to Completion in Christ through Healing Prayer*. Grand Rapids, MI: Baker Books, 1991.

———. *The Healing Presence: Curing the Soul through Union with Christ*. Grand Rapids, MI: Hamewith Books, 1989.

Rahula, Walpola Sri, *What the Buddha Taught*. Oxford: Oneworld Publications, 1997.

Sayers, Dorothy L., "The Other Six Deadly Sins." In *Letters to a Diminished Church: Passionate Arguments for the Relevance of Christian Doctrine*. Nashville: W Publishing Group, 2004.

Bibliography

Smith, Alex G., *A Christian's Pocket Guide to Buddhism*. Fearn, Scotland: Christian Focus Publications, 2009.

Tozer, A. W. *The Knowledge of the Holy*. San Francisco: HarperSanFrancisco, 1961.

The NIV Study Bible. London: Hodder & Stoughton, 1985.

Secular Buddhism UK, "2011 Census Statistics," December 2011. No pages. Online: www.secularbuddhism.co.uk/2012/12/2011-census-statistics/.

Wikipedia, "Religion in the United Kingdom," February 2014. No pages. Online: http://en.wikipedia.org/wiki/Religion_in_the_United_Kingdom.

Wikipedia, "Buddhism in the United States," February 2014. No pages/ Demographics of Buddhism in the United States/Numbers of Buddhists. Online: http://en.wikipedia.org/wiki/Buddhism_in_the_United_States.

Wikipedia, "List of Religious Populations," February 2014. No pages. Online: http://en.wikipedia.org/wiki/Talk:List_of_religious_populations.

FURTHER READING

Baker, Esther. *I Once was a Buddhist Nun*. Nottingham, England: InterVarsity Press, 2009, is also published in Polish, German, Dutch, and Finnish (please see "Helpful Websites" for more details)

Cunningham, Loren. *The Book That Transforms Nations: The Power of the Bible to change any Country*. Seattle, WA: YWAM Publishing, 2007.

Netland, Harold A., and Keith E. Yandell. *Spirituality Without God: Buddhist Enlightenment and Christian Salvation*. Milton Keynes, UK: Authentic Media, 2009.

Pullinger, Jackie. *Chasing the Dragon*. Hodder and Stoughton, 1980.

———. *Crack in the Wall: Life and Death in Kowloon Walled City*. London: Hodder and Stoughton, 1989.

Made in the USA
Lexington, KY
25 July 2017